T0256481

Auditing Cloud Computing

Auditing Cloud Computing

A Security and Privacy Guide

BEN HALPERT

John Wiley & Sons, Inc.

Published by John Wiley & Sons, Inc., Hoboken, New Jersey.
Published simultaneously in Canada.

For general information on our other products and services or for technical support, please contact our Customer Care Department within the United States at (800) 762-2974, outside the United States at (317) 572-3993 or fax (317) 572-4002.

Wiley also publishes its books in a variety of electronic formats. Some content that appears in print may not be available in electronic books. For more information about Wiley products, visit our web site at www.wiley.com.

Library of Congress Cataloging-in-Publication Data

Auditing cloud computing: a security and privacy guide/[edited by] Ben Halpert.
    p. cm. — (Wiley corporate F & A; 21)
      ISBN 978-0-470-87474-5 (pbk); 978-1-118-11602-9 (ebk);
    978-1-118-11603-6 (ebk); 978-1-118-11604-3 (ebk)
  1. Business enterprises—Computer networks—Security measures. 2. Cloud computing—Security measures. 3. Information technology—Security measures.
  4. Data protection. I. Halpert, Ben, 1986-
    HF5548.37.A93 2011
    005.8—dc22

To my wife, for her love, patience, and unwavering support of all my endeavors.

Contents

Preface

A S A KEYNOTE AND session speaker at over 30 conferences to date, I am often asked for references regarding the topics I present. Experience has taught me that it is always best to have the references ready when asked. In 2009, I presented a session on cloud computing at the MIS Training Institute's 29th Annual IT Audit & Controls conference. The room included an audience of very attentive and eager attendees. During my presentation, I discussed the history of cloud computing, the different types of clouds, the rationale as to why organizations are so eager to move to the cloud, challenges of cloud computing, and considerations for leveraging cloud services. When addressing the section on the challenges of cloud computing, I reviewed properties of the cloud along with risks, security, and interoperability aspects. While discussing these topics, I talked about aspects that IT auditors need to consider when conducting an audit of cloud providers.

Throughout the session, there was great interaction among the attendees. During the question and answer segment, at the end, one attendee asked if I could recommend a book or other reference that IT auditors could leverage to increase their knowledge base related to cloud computing topics. At the time there were no such resources, so I responded that I was unaware of such materials targeted specifically at the IT audit community: hence, the origin of the idea for this book.

What you will find in the forthcoming chapters of this text is a collection of white papers written by thought leaders in the space of auditing cloud computing. *Auditing Cloud Computing: A Security and Privacy Guide* can be used in various ways, by a variety of audiences.

First, the chapters are arranged in an order that allows for a logical flow of information providing a comprehensive background in the subject matter. From an introduction to cloud computing, through governance, audit, legal, service delivery, and other perspectives, a holistic view of the cloud computing space is delineated. Second, this text can be used as a reference for specific aspects of cloud computing and questions that may arise during preparation of an audit program or throughout the course of an audit or assessment. Third, the material can support those individuals who want to learn more about the impact of cloud computing on the field of IT audit in support of industry certifications, such as the Certified Information Systems Auditor (CISA) credential, among others. Additionally, this compilation also addresses auditing the cloud from more than simply an auditor's perspective; it provides perspectives from both the cloud provider and the cloud service customer.

What you will *not* find in this book are specific technical controls or audit programs for various point technology solutions that enable the existence of cloud services. Developers of such solutions provide (or should provide!) configuration and hardening guides that can be referenced depending on the environment under consideration. Such specific configuration aspects will change with each code release or product update.

CONTENT DELINEATION

The individual contributors to this text have labored to provide insight, based on their real-world experience, into many aspects that organizations will encounter during their foray into the cloud. The forthcoming chapters exemplify their vast knowledge of the subject matter. You will notice that in many of the chapters certain topics are revisited from the specific author's perspective (introductory material and organizations working the cloud space, as examples). This is not an error or oversight in the content of this text. Rather, it is meant to show the variation in the industry on perception and reality you may and will encounter.

In the first chapter, Omkhar Arasaratnam provides an introduction to the concepts involved in cloud computing. The chapter starts with a brief history into the origins of cloud computing and then introduces relevant definitions. Next, the different types of cloud categories are discussed followed by a review of roles and deployment models in the cloud space. You will notice that care is taken to address aspects not only of cloud consumers, but providers and integrators as well. This is a theme that continues throughout the chapters (although the specific terminology may deviate slightly based on an individual subject matter expert's experience in the industry). The chapter concludes with a discussion of cloud challenges that are then expounded upon in later chapters.

Chapter 2, Cloud-Based IT Audit Process, authored by Jeremy Rissi and Sean Sherman, serves as a gateway to the other chapters by providing an overview of what organizations can expect when creating audit programs for cloud environments. An overview of industry efforts, such as CSA, NIST, ISACA, and ENISA is provided in relation to security and compliance programs. Recommended controls and then a discussion of risk management follow the overview.

As explained by the authors, before an organization should even consider utilizing cloud services, a governance model must be established. In Chapter 3, Mike Whitman and Herb Mattord provide an introduction to governance in the cloud. They then provide guidance on implementing, extending, and maintaining a governance program for cloud activities.

In Chapter 4, System and Infrastructure Lifecycle Management for the Cloud, Steve Riley explores traditional lifecycle management techniques as applied to cloud deployments. Lifecycle management has to be adapted for the cloud due to the fact that processes that were once handled by a single organization will now be shared or handed over completely, depending on the environment. Steve illustrates how existing lifecycle controls can be leveraged. A discussion on cross-cloud deployments follows and the chapter concludes with a cloud service provider's perspective along with a look into what control questions really count.

Peter Coffee then takes us through Cloud-Based IT Delivery and Support in Chapter 5. The concepts of *radical simplification* and *securely shared* are introduced. These concepts apply to all cloud deployment models, even private clouds. Architecture considerations for cloud service delivery and support are discussed in connection with the aforementioned tenets.

In Chapter 6, Protection and Privacy of Information Assets in the Cloud, Nikhil Kumar and Leon DuPree introduce us to the Cloud Security Continuum. The authors then map cloud characteristics against protection and privacy of information assets. A brief discussion of various aspects of regulation and compliance are then considered (more on regulatory and compliance in Chapter 8). The concept of *the playbook* is then introduced and expounded upon.

In Chapter 7, Business Continuity and Disaster Recovery, Jeff Fenton discusses Business Continuity Planning (BCP) and Disaster Recovery Planning (DRP) in general terms and then focuses on the impact of cloud computing that can be augmented to traditional BCP and DRP. Jeff concludes the chapter with specific aspects to consider when utilizing cloud services.

Global Regulation and Cloud Computing, Chapter 8, is authored by Jeremy Rissi and Sean Sherman. The authors provide background into regulations with which organizations must comply, along with cloud-specific considerations. We are presented with the realities of leveraging the cloud, given the global context of an evolving regulatory environment along with aspects for auditors to consider.

Liam Lynch and Tammi Hayes present the final chapter of the book, Cloud Morphing: Shaping the Future of Cloud Computing Security and Audit. As you will notice when reading the chapter, Liam is an active and founding member of the Cloud Security Alliance and the leader of the Trusted Cloud Initiative. The basic premise of the chapter is that change is a constant in the IT industry and organizations and cloud service providers have to morph in order to provide specified levels of assurance for specific data. This industry evolution will allow for effective audit and compliance for business processes in the cloud.

* * *

I would like to express my gratitude to all the contributors who believed in the vision for this book and the need to support the IT audit community. Thank you to Brian Curtis for his guidance throughout the process and to Ronny Nussbaum for his critical eye. A special *thank-you* to Sheck Cho of John Wiley & Sons, Inc., for reaching out to get this project launched. Additionally, the professionalism displayed by Stacey Rivera, Jennifer MacDonald, Natasha Andrews-Noel, Helen Cho and the rest of the John Wiley & Sons, Inc. team made for a pleasurable journey.

Ben Halpert
Atlanta, GA
June 2011

CHAPTER ONE

Introduction to Cloud Computing

Omkhar Arasaratnam

C LOUD COMPUTING HAS taken the IT world by storm. Often viewed as the utopia of utility computing, cloud computing offers flexibility and financial benefits second to none. It also lowers the entry point to high performance computing, allowing organizations to leverage computing power that they have neither the capital budget nor operational expertise to acquire. This chapter provides background as to where cloud computing came from, what cloud computing is, and discusses some of the advantages and challenges with cloud computing.

HISTORY

Computing has evolved significantly over the last 60 years. In the early days, a large central computer would be used by an entire company. This gradually evolved to departmental computers in the 1970s and later personal computers in the 1980s and 1990s. Although cloud computing is a new term, as a concept it was predicted by computer scientist John McCarthy in the

1960s. McCarthy asserted: "Computation may someday be organized as a public utility."

McCarthy had the foresight to predict what we today refer to as cloud computing. In the mid-1960s, Intel co-founder Gordon E. Moore famously predicted that the number of transistors (or computing power) that could be inexpensively placed on an integrated circuit would double every two years. This is commonly known as Moore's law. By the late 1990s, Moore's law had guided computing to heights beyond many organizations' predictions. Much of this demand was fueled by the now popular World Wide Web (WWW), which brought an age of networking and collaboration that had not been seen before.

By the mid-2000s, many companies had discovered that their largest IT purchases were often left idle and only fully utilized during peak demand. These organizations were very large IT or academic organizations. This had researchers wondering how best to leverage the latent processing power. Thus, the initial underpinnings of cloud computing were born.

In 2007, Google, IBM, Carnegie Mellon, MIT, Stanford University, UC Berkeley, the University of Maryland, and the University of Washington collaborated to begin research into cloud computing. Before long, many analyst groups began reporting on the significant market share being established by cloud computing. Many standards organizations and consortiums such as the Open Group, OASIS, and DMTF had also begun working groups to define cloud computing standards.

DEFINING CLOUD COMPUTING

Cloud computing is regarded as an evolutionary rather than a revolutionary step. In other words, cloud computing hasn't drastically altered existing technologies, but rather it has succeeded as a result of the collaboration of several existing technologies.

The actual definition of cloud computing is frequently contested. Most will agree that any computing model that qualifies as cloud computing must at minimum have the following criteria:

Elasticity

Cloud computing is typified by its ability to rapidly scale the capacity of the provided service up or down with little to no interaction from the consumer. This characteristic, known as *elasticity*, is key to cloud computing.

In some delivery models of cloud computing, elasticity is often facilitated through virtualization, although cloud computing does not require virtualization.

Multitenancy

Clouds are inherently multitenanted—even private clouds, which run the workload of a single corporation posses multiple tenants, be they workloads or individual users. This multitenancy and multitenant amortization of the shared compute resource is part of the reason for the economic benefits of cloud computing.

Economics

With cloud computing services, the expectation is that the consumer is charged for the amount of time used on the resource. Cloud computing changes the computing barrier to entry for high performance computing resources, by allowing consumers to use only what they need for the time in which they need it. In turn, this has allowed organizations to effectively respond to peak demand requirements without having excess compute resources sitting idle during dormant periods. Clouds can achieve this by distributing the load across multiple shared resources and relying on economies of scale.

Abstraction

The most significant change with cloud computing is that of abstraction. As we will describe in the following section, most cloud providers provide one or more service layers to their consumers. The operational aspect of the layers supporting the service is insulated from the customer. So, a Software as a Service (SaaS) customer will interact with the application itself, but not with the operating system or hardware of the respective cloud. This key difference allows organizations that do not have the necessary system administration skills or compute facilities to leverage enterprise applications hosted by others.

Many of the technologies that assist in providing these capabilities have been present for many years. Virtualization and autonomic response are areas of computing that have been well understood for decades, as has the Internet. Providers of cloud computing were able to assemble these disparate technologies into the above capabilities, ultimately defining cloud computing.

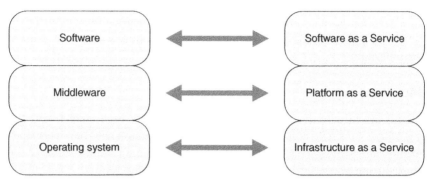

EXHIBIT 1.1 Traditional Model versus Cloud Computing Model

CLOUD COMPUTING SERVICES LAYERS

Cloud computing providers provide different kinds of services to cloud computing consumers. In order to understand the different layers of service, it's
important to understand how they would relate in a noncloud computing
scenario. See Exhibit 1.1.

The kind of service being provided has many implications on the provider,
including how they address concerns such as security, resiliency, compliance,
and multitenancy. Cloud computing services fall into one of the following
categories, as shown in Exhibit 1.2.

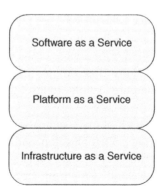

EXHIBIT 1.2 Categories of Cloud Computing Services

Infrastructure as a Service

Infrastructure as a Service (IaaS) providers allow their customers access to different kinds of infrastructure. The provider typically provides this service by dividing a very large physical infrastructure resource into smaller virtual resources for access by the consumer. Sometimes the service provided is a complete virtual machine with an operating system. In other instances the service provided is simply for storage, or perhaps a bare virtual machine with no operating system. In cases where the operating system or other software is included, the cost of the required license is either amalgamated into the cost for the service, or included as an additional surcharge.

IaaS providers are often service providers to other cloud providers (see Integrator). Many current Platform as a Service providers leverage IaaS providers for extra capacity on demand. One of the more popular IaaS providers is Amazon, who provides their EC2 IaaS.

Platform as a Service

Platform as a Service (PaaS) providers extend the software stack provided by IaaS to include *middleware*. Middleware generically refers to software such as a DB2 database, or runtime environments such as a Java Runtime Environment (JRE) or a Websphere application server. This middleware is a prerequisite to running more sophisticated applications, and provides a rich operating environment for the application to exploit. PaaS providers have two methods in which they facilitate the extra capacity needed for a large multitenant system. In some cases, they provide IaaS style virtual machines to the consumer. In other cases they provide an interface through which applications in the case of a runtime environment, or data in the case of a database, can be uploaded. A popular example of a PaaS is Microsoft's Windows Azure platform.

Each method has its advantages and challenges. With an IaaS style approach, the provider typically has more control and stronger separation between tenants. This approach is less efficient, however, as common overhead such as the operating system and the virtual machine itself are duplicated across multiple tenants.

In the second case, the underlying infrastructure is addressed in a much more efficient manner, with a single system image and middleware overhead amortized amongst multiple clients. Conversely, the main challenge with this approach lies in the degree of separation that can be provided between tenants. A runtime environment that is not robust or a misconfigured database can allow one user to adversely affect the quality of service of other users.

Software as a Service

Application as a Service, or Software as a Service (SaaS) providers as they are more commonly known, typically provide a rich web-based interface to their customers. The customer, in most cases, is completely abstracted from the nuances of the application running behind the scenes. Tenant separation is often done at the application layer, leaving a common application, platform, and infrastructure layer underneath. Popular examples of SaaS include Google Apps and Salesforce.com.

SaaS providers typically increase the capacity of their systems through scale up or scale out methods—depending on the characteristics of the application. SaaS applications that scale up are usually moved to larger platforms as their capacity requirements grow. SaaS applications that scale out are typically run on large clusters of servers. As additional capacity is required, the provider adds additional machines to the cluster.

As there is a significant amount of shared resources used between tenants in an SaaS environment, the ability of one tenant to affect the quality of service of other tenants is always a concern. The ability for an SaaS provider to adequately *fence* or insulate one tenant from another is key to maintaining quality of service.

ROLES IN CLOUD COMPUTING

The cloud-computing paradigm defines three key roles. These roles each have different responsibilities and expectations relative to one another. Any party might have multiple roles depending on the context. See Exhibit 1.3.

Consumer

Simply defined, a consumer consumes any service that is provided. In Exhibit 1.3, the SaaS provider exposes an SaaS to the SaaS consumer. The consumer is permitted access to this service for a fee of some sort, though in many instances this fee is augmented or replaced through advertising revenue. The consumer has no responsibility, nor access beyond the SaaS provided to them.

Provider

The providers in this case are both the PaaS provider and the SaaS provider. The PaaS provider provides a PaaS to the SaaS provider. The SaaS provider in

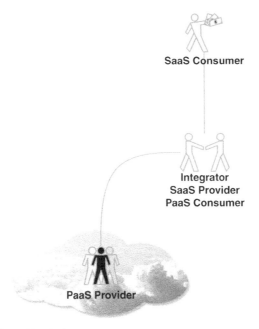

EXHIBIT 1.3 Three Key Roles

turn provides an SaaS to the consumer. Ultimately, the provider is anyone who provides a service to one or more consumers.

Integrator

The integrator role is sometimes referred to as a broker. The integrator essentially assembles the services of many providers under a new service. In some cases, this might involve integrating multiple providers of the same service—for example, the integration of multiple IaaS providers to provide a more resilient or fully-featured IaaS service. In other cases, per our diagram, the integrator might consume another provider's service (in this case PaaS) in order to run a service of their own. The integrator's service is ultimately exposed as an SaaS to the SaaS consumer.

Depending on the perspective, we will see that each party can have multiple roles. The SaaS provider is ultimately a consumer of the PaaS provider, and an integrator of the PaaS service with its SaaS.

CLOUD COMPUTING DEPLOYMENT MODELS

Cloud computing has a number of different deployment models. A deployment model is a particular method of delivering a service. In the case of cloud computing, these are unique methods of deploying a cloud computing service. Deployment models often have particular characteristics that suit them to appropriate workloads. The most commonly used deployment models are as follows.

Private

In a private cloud, the cloud computing services are provided by an internal organization for use by other internal organizations. The provider in this case is most often the internal Information Technology (IT) or Information Systems (IS) department.

Consumers vary, but typically these consumers are consumers of other IT services. As both the consumer and provider are internal organizations, private clouds allow the consumer greater control over quality of service provided by the cloud. For instance, an internal customer can more easily assert the relative priority of a particular workload. In another instance, the internal consumer might assert specific characteristics regarding how critical the workload is, and therefore, the availability requirements of the cloud.

Private clouds generally provide the most control, as both provider and consumer are part of the same organization. This control comes at a price, as the organization ultimately bears the full cost of the cloud infrastructure.

Community

Community clouds have membership in one or more organizations. Community clouds are often groups of individuals and organizations collaborating for the purpose of a particular mission or concern. This might be an industry consortium, an awareness group, or another group altogether. In some instances the community cloud is a shared responsibility, either financially or from a compute resource perspective. In other instances, one member of the community provides all the funding and resources with other members contributing as appropriate. The defining factor for the community cloud is that the different constituents are all assembled for a common cause. As community clouds are provided and supported by consortia with a common cause, there is some influence that members have over the quality of service. The ultimate decision usually applies to the majority and/or veto members.

Public

Public clouds are clouds where the provider delivers a cloud service to any customer who wishes to access it. Unlike a private or community cloud, there are no stipulations regarding the consumer's ownership or cause in using the cloud; it is simply provided for any customer who wishes to support the payment model. One challenge of public clouds is the assurances regarding quality of service. In many instances, today's cloud providers offer little in compensation for missed service level agreements (SLAs). Most often, the only compensation offered is the reimbursement of fees paid by the consumer. For many organizations, the business impact of application downtime can be magnitudes above the cost of the cloud service. Consider the extreme example of a stock exchange where downtime is measured in millions of dollars per hour versus a cloud service measured in cents per hour. This has caused many organizations to avoid using public clouds for their mission-critical workloads, and instead to relegate their usage to noncritical assets.

Further concerns regarding security issues, such as data residency requirements, have prevented the adoption of public cloud computing across some countries. When leveraging public clouds, consumers should exercise due diligence to ensure that their use of the cloud does not violate legislative, regulatory, or industry requirements.

Hybrid

Hybrid clouds are not a separate deployment model, but rather an intersection of two or more—for example, a private SaaS application that is based on a public IaaS.

Hybrid clouds are usually focused on leveraging the economies of scale present in public cloud offerings, but also on driving workloads that have more stringent quality of service requirements. For this reason, in many cases hybrid clouds are internal clouds, which turn to the capacity of public clouds for peak demand.

CHALLENGES

Although there are many benefits to cloud computing, it is not without its own challenges. Traditional computing models have permitted a high degree of control over compute resources. Cloud computing, by virtue of abstraction, prevents the consumer from having the same level of influence over the computing resource.

Of great concern is the ability of consumers to assert quality of service. Quality of service refers to aspects of a service that are not functional (press the red button to submit your form) but are important considerations—for example, how quickly the form submission takes to process. This leads to some of the following challenges with public cloud computing.

Availability

One of the cited benefits to cloud computing is the lowered barrier to entry. This is facilitated financially by sharing a significant amount of infrastructure between consumers. This allows for economies of scale from both a service management and computing resource perspective. Unfortunately, this also causes challenges regarding system availability.

A nefarious user within the cloud can adversely affect the performance or availability of other consumers by attempting to over-consume resources. A similar effect can be attained by using the significant elasticity of the cloud to launch a denial of service attack against other consumers or organizations.

Although most cloud providers have methods of defending against these attacks launched by criminals, law enforcement can be just as disruptive. Consider a recent case where law enforcement officials confiscated racks of servers out of a data center as a result of alleged illegal activity from one of the consumers. Unfortunately, due to the use of virtualization many tenants' information was confiscated at the same time.

Equally significant, in late 2007, Rackspace suffered a 36-hour outage due to a damaged transformer outside of their data centers. This was a significant issue that affected all of its customers.

Cloud consumers should continue to consider availability requirements as well as business continuity plans when using cloud computing. Cloud computing does not alleviate these requirements.

Private cloud users are equally susceptible to this challenge. In scenarios where the directive is to migrate all workloads to a single data center, or to leverage virtual machines over separate physical machines, IT departments may inadvertently increase their single points of failure. This occurs as critical infrastructures are moved to a common area, or previously redundant systems are shifted onto single pieces of hardware.

Data Residency

Different countries and regions have different requirements regarding how its citizens' information should be handled. In some areas, such as the European

Union (EU), there are specific requirements regarding protection of personally identifiable information (PII) of EU residents. In other areas, such as the United States (US), there are directives regarding protected health information (PHI), such as the Health Insurance Portability and Accountability Act (HIPAA).

The challenge is that without knowing where all the cloud provider's assets reside, it is difficult to know with which legislation the consumer needs to comply. Furthermore, if the cloud provider has multiple centers worldwide, in many instances it is impossible to tell where in the world a particular consumer data set might be at any one point in time.

Cloud consumers should consult with their providers regarding the countries in which they operate, and if possible restrict them to a subset that is congruent with their security and compliance requirements.

Multitenancy

Although multitenancy affords cloud consumers unprecedentedly low prices, security and compliance considerations need to be taken into account. Depending on the layer of cloud service being provided, the appropriate security controls should be employed. This can include host intrusion detection systems (HIDS), hypervisor based security agents, host firewalls, and many others.

Some cloud providers will enforce particular controls on their consumers to ensure a minimal level of security. Others will allow their clients full flexibility.

Cloud consumers who have concerns regarding the security of their workload in a multitenant environment should consult their provider regarding their security standards. If the provider's standards are deemed insufficient the consumer should augment this with compensating controls, or defer to an alternate provider.

Depending on the layer of cloud service provided, multitenancy can sometimes cause challenges with obtaining audit logs. Audit logs in a multitenant environment might contain other tenant information, which may or may not be cleansed properly prior to release. If specific audit logging requirements need to be met, the consumer should validate what the provider is capable of providing.

Performance

Many cloud providers assert a particular level of performance based on the service purchased. The main challenge regarding performance is the customer's recourse for degraded performance.

The penalty in an SLA provided by most cloud providers, more often than not, entails a refund of fees for services rendered. For many IaaS services, this is measured in cents per hour. There is no consideration given to the business impact of the service degradation, which may be many orders of magnitude higher. Consider a cloud consumer who might, in turn, provide a stock trading service to their customers with SLA penalties measured in thousands of dollars per second; in such a case, the penalty offered by the cloud provider is wholly inadequate.

Data Evacuation

In cloud environments, data evacuation can be a significant concern. Data evacuation focuses on how sensitive information is cleared from physical storage due to the suspension or deletion of a consumer's resources. This might be a table in a database, a virtual disk on a Storage Area Network (SAN), or virtual memory on a suspended disk. In the highly elastic world of cloud computing, memory is usually de-allocated, but not cleared. So a virtual machine containing sensitive information wouldn't be *zeroed out* prior to deletion, but rather its disk space would be released back to the SAN as is.

Depending on the consumer's requirement regarding data security, this might be a point of concern. Consumers should discuss this requirement if applicable with their provider. In instances where providers do not have advanced capabilities, the consumer should employ their own controls, such as encryption, when possible.

Supervisory Access

One of the main challenges with public cloud computing is that the highest level of access to the system, supervisory access, is maintained by the cloud provider. A cloud provider can inspect the activities of every virtual machine in an IaaS cloud. An SaaS provider has access to the information of all tenants in their cloud.

This is an important consideration for cloud consumers, especially as it pertains to the storage of highly regulated, confidential, proprietary, or other information deemed appropriate for a limited audience.

In such scenarios, it is recommended that the consumer seek contractual obligations and potentially define specific controls for the provider to prevent undue exposure as well as an agreed upon response in the event of an exposure.

 **IN SUMMARY**

Cloud computing is the latest evolution in the delivery of computing power. It lowers the point of entry, permitting access to computing power previously only available to the largest organizations. It also permits smaller organizations to leverage fully-managed computing infrastructures, reducing the requirements for highly skilled IT staff.

Cloud computing is not without its challenges. Sensitive workloads that have strict quality of service requirements may not be appropriate for deployment to the cloud. Of particular concern are workloads with strict security and compliance requirements.

As cloud providers evolve their service offerings to the subsequent generations of the cloud, more sensitive workloads may eventually be permitted to leverage the advantages of cloud computing.

CHAPTER TWO

Cloud-Based IT Audit Process

Jeremy Rissi
Sean Sherman

T HE CLOUD SUPPORTS a business model with some significant benefits for the consumer, including cost savings for equipment and for management of Information Technology (IT) resources and business services. Examples such as e-mail and office applications, sales/customer management and payroll services, and infrastructure on demand have all been successfully implemented via cloud services by a number of companies and agencies. But there are security risks exacerbated by outsourcing to the cloud that have not been fully understood by either buyers or providers of cloud services, that are important to consider, especially as it comes to compliance and regulation.

It is not unusual that decisions to use the cloud are initially driven by economic desires and not as part of an IT and business services roadmap. When cost savings drive business decisions, it is critical that concerns about meeting regulatory requirements not be an afterthought, or worse, not considered until the auditors arrive. Worse yet, changes to IT infrastructure that are not understood by the business can introduce significant risk to the business itself, and so audit, compliance, and risk management should all be considered part of the true cost of cloud computing.

This chapter reviews the audit approach and unique concerns in assuring security and compliance in the cloud environment. We discuss the common failing of security when a business starts to use the cloud and the types of controls that would be most important to use when assurance is needed. This is valuable information to the system owner and operations staff because it will help to explain the changes to risk and security that should be addressed by moving applications and data to the cloud. The system owner and operator should exert themselves to understand the perspective of security practitioners and auditors, and consider control frameworks in the context of current IT security and compliance programs. For instance, it is common that security controls inherent to a corporate network convey to a system residing on that network, but they typically do not convey to a system residing in the cloud. Security controls must move toward the data and applications to be effective in the cloud.

The IT audit perspective helps organizations to clarify the compliance risk and security risk to their systems. The value of understanding both concerns can reduce costs, improve security, and make cloud computing successful.

THE AUDIT PROCESS

What is audit? Audit is essentially an assurance function that some standard, method, or practice is followed. Depending on the type of audit, the auditor systematically examines evidence for compliance to established criteria. The best practice in effective IT auditing is to start with an understanding of business functions, to identify which IT infrastructure is providing those functions, and to then consider the scope of the audit and controls best suited for that IT function. The same holds true for IT infrastructure and services provided by the cloud. In fact, most cloud providers are using IT systems models similar to those of their clients. These include: securing workstation (access) and server devices, core services (such as identity and authorization), and monitoring and logging functions. Therefore, many of the same controls and control frameworks (like COBIT or NIST) typically used for systems audits are also usable for auditing systems that are hosted or provided by cloud vendors.

But as businesses move into cloud environments, certain changes occur that auditors must recognize as the move changes the scope of the audit and introduces new risk to systems. Cloud architectures are different from systems hosted by traditional infrastructure and auditors should pay close attention to these types of situations:

- When an IT service or function is moved to the cloud from an existing internal model, the controls that protected it may not move to the cloud. For example, a system that was protected by strong controls provided by the corporate local area network (LAN) can lose those controls when that system is hosted by a cloud vendor. In typical corporate systems, it is not uncommon that data is not encrypted and applications are not using strong authentication or access controls. These internal systems could rely on network access controls and private corporate networks for security. If this same data is moved to the cloud, it now passes over the Internet. These applications, if not adapted for the cloud, can now be compromised by lack of secure authentication controls and data integrity issues for data at rest or in transit.
- Systems that are developed in-house expecting a level of security provided by the corporate network are similarly at risk when moved to a cloud provider. For instance, custom applications are typically not extensively tested for common Internet vulnerabilities before hosted on internal networks or portals, but in a public setting could be vulnerable to a variety of security incidents such as data breaches, cross-site scripting, hacking, botnets, and worms. Public, web accessible applications must be carefully developed and tested before made available to assure appropriate access, authentication, and monitoring.
- Identity management, where users are authenticated and authorized through a single centrally controlled service model (e.g., Active Directory), can become much more intricate and new risks may be introduced due to that complexity. Some cloud environments can introduce greater-than-typical access controls, but these should be tested to auditor satisfaction.
- Endpoint security becomes more important for systems that no longer have or expect network firewalls. A common scenario exists in which work-stations turn off firewall services because they expect they are protected within the corporate infrastructure—and these systems are compromised to gain "legitimate" access to cloud resources.
- Cloud servers maintained by a vendor are patched and tested in a generic manner, but can cause failure or inadvertent risk to custom systems. Close interaction with cloud vendors to assure that new risks are not introduced as a result is needed.

▪ Cloud environments—regardless of hybrid, community, public, or private models—introduce an essential change in audit scope of network boundary. Careful inspection of communications between vendor and corporate environments is required. Typically, this will call for enhanced monitoring of communications controls.

Most auditors will find that audit of cloud infrastructure should be similar to audit of localized internal infrastructure but will have some uniquely important control areas: those that control access, authorization, and trusted control frameworks. The auditor must consider the business function that is being supported by the IT services or system that is being moved into the cloud. Questions about communications latency, data breach notification, and international laws (where the provider infrastructure moves data between international data centers) are all new potential issues for the cloud-hosted system. Auditors should study cloud solutions carefully since effective audits, including appropriate scope and controls, will be unique to each system.

Audit in the cloud does have similar issues to standard infrastructure auditing that should be considered—such as clearly addressing conflict of interest and independence of the auditor, professional auditing practices and adequate technical training and proficiency of the auditor, and audit reports that clearly assert findings and qualified opinions-based evidence and documentation.

Audit will be different for the cloud depending on the deployment model of cloud outsourcing (private, public, community, or hybrid) and service model Software as a Service [SaaS], Infrastructure as a Service [IaaS], Platform as a Service [PaaS]. The essential differences will be most evident in the public and hybrid types of clouds—as these will rely most heavily on contracts and (possibly complex) agreements and compliance to those agreements. And because the use of the cloud implies the use of the Internet and "extension" of the corporate network, all cloud models vary in features and controls that must be considered while planning and executing an audit.

CONTROL FRAMEWORKS FOR THE CLOUD

When adopting new technology of any kind, both system owners and internal auditors must consider not only the business justification for adoption but also the risks inherent to the new technology. Control (compliance) frameworks have not yet been well adapted to cloud environments, although most (like COBIT, ITIL, and ISO 27001) are considered sufficient overall and a worthy starting point. There are organizations that have been instrumental in exploring the cloud in relation to security and compliance programs—the most active are currently CSA, NIST, ISACA, and ENISA.[1] These organizations have been leading the development of concepts and guidance sufficient to understand, protect, and trust cloud infrastructure. It is advisable to keep up with new publications from these organizations (and many others) to keep abreast of new thought and advice.

The most consistent advice from most of these organizations focuses on some core concepts, which include:

- ▪ Cloud hosted/based systems cannot be protected in the same manner as traditional corporate systems. In most cases, security controls (compliance objectives—from an audit perspective) must be moved closer to the system and its data.
- ▪ Auditors may find that they are addressing control buildup—likely to occur since it is difficult to stop traditional controls without strong justification. However, overprescribed controls are wasteful of time and resources, so it is important to remove those controls that are no longer relevant or appropriate.
- ▪ New controls or enhanced reliance on core security services such as log/ event monitoring, identity management, physical security, and virtual server technology may require a sophisticated understanding of technology previously unnecessary for auditors.
- ▪ A strong understanding of network scope is required for most cloud audits. Topology of the cloud environment will include the changes to the corporate system, links to hosted systems, partner connections, and complexity introduced with cloud-vendors-to-the-cloud-vendor (hybrid) environments.

Some strategies to address these issues include leaning on the cloud vendors themselves to put their systems into a trusted, monitored, and certified state. Many cloud vendors have started with SAS 70 or SSAE 16 audits, but these are traditionally insufficient for a strong level of trust and assurance. More recently, vendors have started to work on specific control frameworks to support the most common compliance domains, such as Payment Card Industry (PCI), Sarbanes-Oxley (SOX), Federal Information Security Act (FISMA), and others. Looking to cloud vendors who have submitted to this type of control documentation and ongoing compliance program support will make an auditor's job of compliance verification much easier.

The following is an assessment of control frameworks or programs that should prove valuable for the auditor or organization that is considering cloud computing and the impacts to their existing control frameworks.

ENISA Cloud Risk Assessment

ENISA is the European Network and Information Security Agency. It is a purely advisory organization, but it has commissioned work on security issues including "Cloud Computing Risk Assessment,"[2] published in November 2009. This paper provided one of the first risk assessments of the cloud computing business model and outlines some evenhanded views on the risks and benefits of cloud computing. In particular, this document provides uniquely specific advice to those organizations that do business in the European Union, or are planning to do so.

One of the key findings of this document was the summary of three recommendations (from a risk standpoint) of the cloud computing models. These were:

1. Building trust in the cloud (a continual issue between vendors and clients)
2. Data protection in largescale environments (incorporating international boundaries, forensics, and incident handling)
3. Engineering (large-scale systems' interoperability, resiliency, and monitoring)

There have been significant efforts on all these fronts by vendors and customers since the publication, which underscores the value of this research.

FedRAMP

The FedRAMP program[3] is worthy of some mention here as a possible model for certification of compliance standards. It is a trust model for U.S. federal agencies to certify and accredit (C&A) cloud providers for FISMA compliance.[4] This program allows vendors to apply for FISMA certification and to be tested and vetted according to NIST 800-53 (rev.3) and other relevant federal guidance. The certification and testing of that environment would be done by the GSA, or another federal agency, which provides the evidence to agencies that the vendor environment meets the federal standard. Then agencies would not have to address some of the audit and expense of federal compliance of hosted systems. Auditors would rely on the certification of the hosted environment and would forgo the independent audit of those environments.

It is an ambitious program that is trying to address some of the concerns addressed in this chapter—and underscores how important trust is for cloud services. For this to work, the vendor becomes a committed partner to meeting standards, monitoring controls, and becoming involved with the security of their clients' systems.

Entities Using COBIT

ISACA is the organization responsible for the control framework COBIT[5]—a readily recognized set of control frameworks for IT systems to meet COSO[6]/SOX requirements and ISO 27001 Information Security Management Systems (ISMS). It defines control objectives that can be refined with risk assessment to describe a specific control or control outcomes. It is a mature framework that has been assessed by many to set standards for governance of IT security. ISACA has released a current guide called "Cloud Computing Management Audit/Assurance Program",[7] which describes an assessment method to use with cloud vendors to assure internal and service provider controls meet control objectives. As expected, this is a sophisticated process to assure both IT framework coverage and quality objectives. It is a good resource for assessment of contractual agreements and control issues found in cloud environments. It does assume, however, that there are governance institutions/mechanisms at the business level.

CSA Guidance

The Cloud Security Alliance (CSA) published Security Guidance for Critical Areas of Focus in Cloud Computing V2.1[8] in December 2009. This work has become well referenced and considered a solid foundation for approaching security in the cloud. The Domain 4 ("Compliance and Audit") section of this document is most applicable to the discussion in this chapter. CSA points out much of the responsibility for compliance to regulations will have to be borne by the consumer, making the consumer responsible for bridging the information and communications gap with audit function. This is true insofar as the business is responsible for planning and meeting compliance, but discounts the role that the vendor can provide. Nonetheless, review the recommendations of this guidance for tips on addressing compliance concerns with vendors, approaches to legal issues, and a reminder that auditors must be qualified to understand some of the security approaches in cloud computing.

CloudAudit/A6—The Automated Audit, Assertion, Assessment, and Assurance API

The CloudAudit/A6 group is a relatively new organization and a public effort to address audit and compliance of cloud services. Merged with CSA in 2011, it endeavors to create a common method for providers of cloud computing services to automate audit functions of their infrastructure—regardless of service type (IaaS, PaaS, or SaaS) and regardless of platform technology.[9]

The goal of this group is to allow cloud consumers to be able to check (audit/assess) remote infrastructure via a common (non-platform-specific) interface/namespace. The advantages of this mechanism would be obvious: Vendors would be able to provide customer access to controls that could meet compliance and security requirements without having to expend as much time on testing and assurance tasks. The consumer and the vendor would not have to specify specific controls if the CloudAudit/A6 efforts are standard—and there could be a mapping of controls to various compliance requirements without having to prescribe specific measures that are platform specific.

This organization has extended an invitation for auditors, vendors and consumers to work together via a forum at their web site. As with similar efforts at building standards for cloud services, the efforts are a work in progress, and it may serve the reader well to stay abreast or to get involved directly.

 RECOMMENDED CONTROLS

Controls should be defined and refined based on the needs of the business, both regulatory and security. Some baseline technical and operational controls are likely to be universally applicable and the following exhibit may assist in helping to consider control areas of comparatively high importance.

Exhibit 2.1 is provided to assist an organization or auditor in consideration of a variety of core control areas and should not be assumed sufficient for any specific security audit. Exhibit 2.1 assumes internal control is a process, designed to provide reasonable assurance regarding the achievement of objectives in the following three categories:

1. Effectiveness and efficiency of operations
2. Reliability of financial reporting
3. Compliance with laws and regulations[10]

EXHIBIT 2.1 Controls—for Cloud Environments

GOVERNMENTAL/HIGHLY SENSITIVE DATA environment

Physical location of data

Data classification (both features and support)

System data isolation (virtual server versus allocated drive)

System resource reuse (erase procedures)

Support or provision for two-factor authentication

Existing certification to security framework (e.g., ISO 27001, FISMA), scope of systems, and protection profile of that certification

PERSONNEL process

Pre-employment check information (identity, nationality or status, employment history and references, criminal convictions, and vetting)

Consistent HR practices (need to be consistent across regions)

Security education program for staff

SUPPLY CHAIN issues

Define key services/products outsourced and provided to operations

Security plan that addresses third-party access to cloud

Audit of third-party providers (frequency, level)

Security policy and controls applied (contractually) to third-party providers

OPERATIONAL environment

Change control process/governance

Remote access policy

System documentation, operating procedures

Test bed

System hardening (technical controls applied to system components)

Anti-virus/white list controls

Mobile device controls

Backup and restore process

Log management

Right to audit provisions

(Continued)

EXHIBIT 2.1 *(Continued)*

SOFTWARE ASSURANCE

Quality Assurance and Quality Control process and procedure

Test plans

PATCH MANAGEMENT

Patch management documentation for all system components and layers of cloud architecture

Test plans

Update logs

NETWORK CONTROLS

Levels of isolation in the architecture

Virtual infrastructure controls

Specific LAN architecture used (e.g., PVLAN, VLAN tagging) and network layer controls used (e.g., DNS control)

Interoperability (service) support

HOST ARCHITECTURE issues

System hardening standard used

Use and protection of the baseline build

Authentication controls

Firewall and IPS settings

Service/management system controls

Virtualized system template controls

Interoperability controls

PAAS—APPLICATION SECURITY

Design of multitenanted application hosting

Access control measures

Vulnerability scanning

Security features

SAAS—APPLICATION SECURITY

Administrative access controls

Customized access control

(Continued)

EXHIBIT 2.1 *(Continued)*

RESOURCE PROVISIONING issues

Overload plan

Exception plan

Lead time on service requests

Virtualization image certification

IDENTITY AND ACCESS MANAGEMENT— AUTHORIZATION

System-wide rights

Account management plan/methodology

Segregation of duties/least privilege rules

Emergency procedures affecting access

User account management (registration included)

ENCRYPTION

Password and key management

Incident management (including emergency and key revocation)

Encryption of data in transit

Encryption of data at rest

Encryption management plan (including emergency management process)

AUTHENTICATION

Authentication plan (relative to client/vendor agreements)

MUTUAL AUTHENTICATION

Mechanism defined and documented

IDENTITY MANAGEMENT FRAMEWORKS

Identity Management infrastructure plan (including providers and features)

CLIENT ACCESS CONTROL

Role-based access control planning for multiple roles and possible multiple domains

Endpoint (customer) system image management

BUSINESS CONTINUITY MANAGEMENT

recovery point objective (RPO) and recovery time objective (RTO) for services

(Continued)

EXHIBIT 2.1 (*Continued*)

Emergency procedures, with details on assets, services, and specific processes

Memos of understanding (MOUs) on emergency procedures

INCIDENT MANAGEMENT AND RESPONSE

Detection capabilities/controls

Communication plan regarding incidents

Forensics plan

Reporting frequency/analysis provided

Privacy controls

PHYSICAL SECURITY issues

Physical protection plan

Compliance level of physical security controls to standards (e.g., FISMA, ISO)

Access control measures

Data destruction process

ENVIRONMENTAL CONTROL issues

Risk management plan

Special controls to address environmental disasters.

LEGAL REQUIREMENTS

Country where cloud provider located (laws and legal agreements)

Country where cloud infrastructure located (laws and legal agreement)

Data ownership/responsibility agreements

Procedures for discovery/e-discovery protections

Regulatory and other compliance requirements

 ## RISK MANAGEMENT AND RISK ASSESSMENT

The cloud user is strongly advised to perform a risk assessment of any system proposed for the cloud environment. In some cases, the assessment of risk will be performed as part of enterprise risk management and should be adjusted to address specific risks associated with different vendors, specific cloud offerings, existing compliance requirements, and data sensitivity.

Risk Management

Because controls cannot be prescriptive beyond a certain baseline, and because all systems are somewhat different, a risk management process component should be developed for most environments to assure the security and compliance of any system. In many organizations, a governance model is advised to help in management of the risk process. In many cases, compliance programs are expecting to find a risk management process that is documented, supported by management, and able to address the risk assessment and configuration control process at a minimum. In any case, cloud computing introduces a variety of risk scenarios that a risk management process is likely to find challenging— such as scope of control, trust (and verification) provisions to contracts, service level agreements (SLAs), and memos of understanding (MOUs). Risk management process documentation should be made available to auditors.

Risk Assessment

A risk assessment is a process wherein the stakeholders try to analyze and agree on a particular threat to a specific system (or component) and the probability of an occurrence. The exercise is sometimes scientific, but often involves an element of guesswork when data points are lacking. For this reason, it is sometimes considered a flawed practice, but it is also the best way to identify and document the threat and mitigation for a particular system at a particular time. The risk assessment itself can be seen as both an activity and a product. The product should be constantly reviewed and protected at the same time. An auditor should be able to review the risk assessment product and observe the risk assessment process.

The consideration of risk management and the risk assessment is suited to a solid discussion during the cloud computing audit. The wide range of unique risks facing the organization make this an important subject and depend on the type and model of the cloud solution, the uniqueness of the client environment, and the specifics of data or an application. As we have pointed out above, many of the risks to cloud environments are similar and in some cases the same as traditionally hosted and outsourced IT systems. The auditor will recall and focus on these common items:

- Gaps in control between processes performed by the service provider and the organization
- Compromises of system security and confidentiality
- Solutions selected incorrectly or with significant missing requirements

- Discrepancies in contracts and gaps between business expectations and service provider capabilities
- Costly compensating controls
- Reduced system availability and questionable integrity of information
- Poor software quality, inadequate testing, and a high number of failures
- Failures to respond to relationship issues with optimal and approved decisions
- Insufficient allocation of resources
- Inability to satisfy audit/assurance charter and requirements of regulators or external auditors
- Fraud

None of these are common controls, and each is likely to require an independent assessment of risk and mitigation by the sourcing firm.

In addition, cloud environments and projects generate new risks due to a number of issues that are somewhat unique to this new computing model. The complexity brought about by dependency on third-party providers brings up unique problems that can be challenging—problems that almost always require specific address: vulnerability of communications channels, external interfaces, and reliance on self-imposed controls. The auditor will often uncover increased risks in cloud data centers because relationships with outside providers are not transparent to his organization. He will grapple with the issues and complexity of local and international laws. Compliance with these laws is difficult, due to the newness of the cloud business model, the potential for data flow through foreign countries, and the likelihood that incident and privacy laws will vary significantly in certain countries. Unique to the industry are a variety of technical challenges with operations that include the needs of the facility to grow rapidly and balance load requirements, the co-location of facilities with other businesses (including competitors), and the untested nature of the business model. The solutions to these issues are typically found in careful planning and recognition that the audit may help you sleep at night.

Legal

Legal agreements are also an important factor in the risk assessment. There are always a number of sources for advice on what should be included in the client-provider agreements to mitigate certain risks, and we agree auditors should inspect these documents as part of their risk review. Organizations such as ENISA and others have done a review of some of the legal issues and some of the advice is worth repeating here. Agreements common to any cloud computing scenario most often address the following issues:

1. *Data protection* requires an understanding of where data is going to reside and what legal protections must be addressed at that residence, especially the privacy and retention conditions. The auditor must make certain that the organization and provider understand what data protections are being promised and what the risks will be to availability and integrity of data.
2. *Confidentiality* is a significant issue when moving data and applications to the cloud. Agreements should address confidentiality, what protections/controls are made against inadvertent release of confidential information, and how classification of data will be supported (when applicable) and managed accordingly.
3. *Intellectual property* is an issue when custom code, data files, and other forms of business data are stored or processed by a cloud provider. Protections should be stated and risks assumed.
4. *Professional negligence* protections must be addressed. Customers must assess risks and possible mitigations that range from insurance to code protection.
5. *Outsourcing services* and changes in control of your cloud provider infrastructure can occur without the client being aware. Agreements must make certain that any change of controls is brought to the attention of the client.

IN SUMMARY

Business today relies on IT. When an IT process incorporates capabilities derived from the cloud, not only are systemic IT risks introduced, but business risks are introduced. The cloud computing environment is a serious change in business service model. In some cases, not all risks can be mitigated. If a risk leads to the failure of a business, serious damage to reputation, or legal implications, it is hard or impossible for any other party to compensate for this damage.[11] So, while the cost benefits of paying for computing utility can be significant, the risks of eating all of the savings away must be carefully assessed. The challenge for businesses will be to remain mindful of the balance between IT risk and business risk.

In order to make an accurate assessment, the cloud computing audit program must adapt to new technology, business models, and processes.

Auditors are faced with the challenge of learning how to use cloud computing, to train and hire appropriately, and to stay abreast of current thought about risk, vulnerabilities, and threats in the cloud. System owners, security practitioners, and auditors alike should study cloud models and the development of new cloud control models being introduced by organizations such as Cloud Security Alliance, NIST, and ISACA. Additionally, it is important that users of any resources continually check up on the respective organization for the most current version and guidance associated with frameworks or standards. Remember that these control models are largely new ground for vendors and businesses trying to work out security and compliance issues in real time.

A corporation or agency should adhere to the basic tenants of auditing when addressing cloud computing. The professional control frameworks should work for cloud environments as they did for hosted and private networks but controls should be closer to the data and applications they host. Access and authorization controls are more important in the semi-public and public cloud environment. Endpoint protection has increased importance.

Only with an investment in the appropriate internal audit of a cloud computing project can an organization effectively achieve balance between business risk and business opportunity.

NOTES

1. See the References section at the end of this chapter.
2. www.enisa.europa.eu/act/rm/files/deliverables/cloud-computing-risk-assessment.
3. www.info.apps.gov is the GSA site on cloud computing. To watch progress of FedRAMP, check www.cio.gov/pages.cfm/page/Federal-Risk-and-Authorization-Management-Program-FedRAMP.
4. FISMA is the Federal Information Security Management Act (2002) and requires all federal IT systems to be certified and accredited to the control framework outlined in NIST 800-37 and 800-53 in particular. This is an intense control framework that often is paperwork and audit intense. It has left federal agencies unclear on how to use cloud computing.
5. ISACA is an international professional association that deals with IT Governance, auditing standards, and professional certification. It was previously known as the Information Systems Audit and Control Association. COBIT stands for Control OBjectives for Information and related Technologies—and is a standard utilized by much of the commercial IT auditing domain. ISACA also authors the ITAF, or the IT Assurance Framework.

6. Committee of Sponsoring Organizations of the Treadway Commission (COSO) Internal Control Framework.
7. www.isaca.org/Knowledge-Center/Research/ResearchDeliverables/Pages/Cloud-Computing-Management-Audit-Assurance-Program.aspx.
8. www.cloudsecurityalliance.org/csaguide.pdf.
9. Review A6/CloudAudit at http://cloudaudit.org/ and also on the CSA web site. Also review effort by NIST to set guidance and standards through recently set up NIST working groups on cloud computing (http://collaborate.nist.gov/twiki-cloud-computing/bin/view/CloudComputing/WebHome).
10. Taken from ECIIA/FERMA—Guidance 8th EU.
11. ENISA: Cloud Computing: Benefits, risks and recommendations for information security, November 2009.

REFERENCES

ENISA. www.enisa.europa.eu/ (accessed March 19, 2011).

Cloud Computing Risk Assessment. 2009. www.enisa.europa.eu/act/rm/files/deliverables/cloud-computing-risk-assessment (accessed March 19, 2011).

Cloud Security Alliance (CSA). http://cloudsecurityalliance.org/ (accessed March 19, 2011).

CSA: Security Guidance for Critical Areas of Focus in Cloud Computing V2.1 (December 2009). https://cloudsecurityalliance.org/csaguide.pdf (accessed March 19, 2011).

CSA Cloud Security Alliance GRC Stack is a link site to CSA tools for audit/compliance and governance. https://cloudsecurityalliance.org/Research.html (accessed March 19, 2011).

U.S. National Institute of Standards and Technology (NIST), web site on cloud computing, including cloud definitions, links to forums, and other cloud security information. http://csrc.nist.gov/groups/SNS/cloud-computing/ (accessed March 19, 2011).

NIST Risk Management Guidance. 2002. http://csrc.nist.gov/publications/nistpubs/800-30/sp800-30.pdf (accessed March 19, 2011).

NIST Recommended Security Controls—FISMA. 2009. http://csrc.nist.gov/publications/nistpubs/800-53-Rev3/sp800-53-rev3-final.pdf (accessed March 19, 2011).

NIST Cloud Computing Working Group(s) have forum and information. http://collaborate.nist.gov/twiki-cloud-computing/bin/view/CloudComputing/WebHome (accessed March 19, 2011).

Public Company Accounting Oversight Board (PCAOB) web site on compliance with SOX and addressing current issues. http://pcaobus.org/Pages/default.aspx (accessed March 19, 2011).

ISACA site for information on the COBIT Framework. www.isaca.org/Knowledge-Center/COBIT/Pages/Overview.aspx (accessed March 19, 2011).

Open Cloud Consortium with information on standards and interoperability for cloud environments. http://opencloudconsortium.org/ (accessed March 19, 2011).

Open Group, standards forum with information on cloud computing issues and guidance. www.opengroup.org/cloudcomputing/ (accessed March 19, 2011).

Open Cloud Computing Interface Working Group with forum and guidance documentation in Wiki. www.occi-wg.org (accessed March 19, 2011).

Open Virtualization Format OVF v1. www.dmtf.org/sites/default/files/standards/documents/DSP0243_1.0.0.pdf (accessed March 19, 2011).

U.S. Federal Government (CIO.GOV) program to support Federal Risk and Authorization Management Program (FedRAMP) cloud trust initiative. www.cio.gov/pages.cfm/page/Federal-Risk-and-Authorization-Management-Program-FedRAMP (accessed March 19, 2011).

A6—The Automated Audit, Assertion, Assessment, and Assurance API forum site (now also through CSA). http://code.google.com/p/cloudaudit/ (accessed March 19, 2011).

FERMA/ECIIA: Guidance for boards and audit committees—8th European Company Law Directive on Statutory Audit DIRECTIVE 2006/43/EC—Art. 41-2b 21 (September 2010). www.eciia.eu/system/files/eccia_ferma_web_1.pdf (accessed March 19, 2011).

CHAPTER THREE

Cloud-Based IT Governance

Mike Whitman
Herb Mattord

Cloud computing is not just a new technology. It is a whole new way of providing IT services to an enterprise. There will be technical, security, privacy, and business process and governance issues to be addressed. The cloud computing FUD factor is still dangerously high. Opportunities may be being missed whilst risks may be improperly addressed. Knowledge is essential. All businesses will need to consider whether or not the cloud is for them. Ignorance or denial can only bring grief.

—*Paul Williams*, ComputerWeekly

C LOUD COMPUTING IS not a new concept; rather, it is a new label for an innovation in networking applied to tried and true outsourcing. Some would say that cloud computing has made the first turn on the hype cycle[1] and is moving into the mainstream. Others disagree, but governing the operations of cloud computing initiatives appears to be in the future of quite a few IT practitioners. Put simply, cloud computing is another way to outsource IT capital goods. Leasing access to advanced technologies is a concept older than the computer itself. Now, however, organizations don't have to host and support the leased technology themselves. Organizations can lease the capability (hardware, operating systems, applications, and support) as needed, paying only the type and quantity of resources necessary to accomplish their business goals. No longer will an organization have banks of computers, servers, and applications running at a fraction of their optimum capacity, representing a dramatically underutilized resource and investment. Cloud computing allows the organization to leverage the development of intellectual property, and take that IP to market using leased technical capabilities.

Cloud computing is often a misunderstood opportunity. There is a lack of standardization in defining it and there is little understanding of how cloud computing can benefit an organization. While being blissfully ignorant may be desirable for a corporate governance team in some aspects of their business, it may be a dangerous state in regards to cloud computing and its security. Unless aggressively managed, cloud computing may move into an organization masquerading as routine contract service arrangements. According to Portio Research[2] over half of IT managers surveyed in Europe knew very little about cloud computing, but that of those who did, over 75 percent were actively involved with cloud computing projects. This means many organizations may be spending on cloud computing without even knowing it, or managing the opportunities and risks of its use.

> The apparent lack of CIO understanding of cloud computing, coupled with another recent survey (from Coleman Parkes for Fujitsu), which indicated that CIOs have a tendency to play safe with proven technology rather than take an informed risk on innovative solutions, does raise questions of governance. With all of the media discussions on cloud computing it is probable that the CIO's boardroom colleagues will at least have heard the term and may be curious about what it means and its potential business benefits.[3]

With the questions raised by the board of directors, CIOs will be called on the carpet to not only explain what cloud computing is, but to also explain why their organization is not deploying it. The difficulty lies in clearly defining and relating the various technologies grouped under the cloud computing umbrella, and identifying reliable vendors and services that would benefit the organization. Then the work really begins, evaluating the costs and benefits, and assessing and evaluating the risks associated with pursuing cloud computing investments.

One of the leading drawbacks, recognized by multiple experts on the subject, is the *trust* of the storage and handling of organizational data by third-party cloud computing vendors. Adding multiple layers of regulation and complexity, if these third-party vendors are across state lines, or even international, the challenges associated with the collection and use of organizational data become dramatically increased indeed. Yet, this is nothing the multi-national organization has not dealt with before.

With the movement of applications and hardware to leased services, the storage, access, and protection of one of the most critical organizational resources is placed in the hands of a company the organization may not know, and certainly will not be able to control beyond the bounds of the lease agreement. Thus, the oversight, management, and control of these agreements becomes the nexus of the governance issues in cloud computing. If the question is not raised by the governing board, it may very well be raised by the organization's shareholders and clientele.

> Most UK businesses (71 percent) think security is the biggest threat to cloud computing, a survey of IT chiefs has found. . . . Over three-quarters of the respondents said they would be concerned if their company's data was stored outside the office. Only 12 percent said they store data in the cloud, therefore if cloud computing is going to take off organizations need strategies that make the cloud more secure. . . . The priority for most companies is to be able to tighten security to the point where they are comfortable to embrace the cloud and maximize its benefits.[4]

In order to manage the risk associated with cloud computing, organizations must formalize their approach to managing the security issues with which it is associated. This requires an investment in time and effort at the top layers of the organization. In other words, it requires governance.

GOVERNANCE IN THE CLOUD

In order to understand the issues facing security in cloud computing, a brief overview of the exact nature and definition of cloud computing is important. To ensure understanding of security and governance issues, one must first speak from a common vocabulary. With the onslaught of discussions, definitions, and proclamations of what cloud computing is, it becomes challenging to relate best practices in security governance to something so ill-understood without standardization.

Understanding the Cloud

Some consider cloud computing a paradigm shift, the next evolution in modern computing infrastructures. One might just consider it an extension of the client-server computing architectures that had the same hype in the 1990s. While very prevalent today, the client-server architecture had to evolve and be adapted to Internet models to gain widespread acceptance.

Client-server computing or the client-server architecture (C/SA) is the distribution of computer processing between multiple systems over a network connection. The four basic functions of the computer, presentation (user interaction), application processing, data access, and data storage, can be distributed within or between multiple systems. This was the approach initially conceived in client-server computing. Modern adaptations of this model have led to interpreting C/SA as the distribution of some function of the system over a network or the Internet. Cloud computing is a physical implementation of this concept using another organization's hardware, software, and infrastructure to provide services to one's constituencies. Cloud computing distributes some or all of the computer processing, hardware, software, and/or infrastructure to a third party for organizational applications. In effect, technology is no longer the focus; it is only a service.

Cloud computing is most commonly described in three offerings:

1. Software as a Service (SaaS), in which applications are provided at a fee but hosted on third-party systems and accessed over the Internet (and the WWW).
2. Platform as a Service (PaaS), in which development platforms are available to developers for a fee and similarly hosted by third parties.
3. Infrastructure as a Service (IaaS) (unofficially known as Everything as a Service) provides hardware and operating systems resources to host

whatever the organization desires to implement, again hosted by a third party for a fee.

Clouds can be public, community, private, or some combination of the three:

1. Public clouds—the most common implementation, where a third party makes the services available to whomever needs them, over the Internet (and WWW).
2. Community clouds—a collaboration between a few entities for the sole benefit of those entities.
3. Private clouds—an extension of the intranet applied to cloud computing, while technically negating the benefits of cloud computing (little or no capital investment), a theoretical implementation could exist where a parent company creates a cloud for it and its subordinate organizations' use.

Security Issues in the Cloud

Corporate concerns over data security are holding back cloud computing. Security experts, software suppliers, and cloud service providers alike see the cloud as a once-in-a-lifetime opportunity to make information security better than ever. The U.S. government's cyber security adviser Howard Schmidt says cloud computing will enable businesses to catch up on security issues and ensure they have the right mechanisms in place going forward.

His enthusiasm offers a sharp contrast to typical cloud computing security debates, which tend to focus on enterprise concerns about cybercriminals exploiting a single point of weakness to steal sensitive information.

Mark Lewis, partner and head of outsourcing at law firm Berwin Leighton Paisner, says that usually the biggest concern with cloud computing is that it puts all a company's data and applications in one place. He points out that in the traditional outsourcing model, the all-in-one-place scenario rarely happens because financial services firms package their contracts with different outsource suppliers.

It is unclear how businesses will follow this strategy in the cloud, but Schmidt believes that, if handled properly, the shift to cloud-based computing could lead to better security. A reliable security infrastructure, says Schmidt, is essential if business is to get the full value out of cloud-based computing. "Because cloud platforms are still developing, we now have the opportunity to build in best practice around things like authentication, data protection, and data disposal from the start," he says.[5]

Alternatively, "when you go to a public space, security is paramount. What do I do with my proprietary information and service levels? How certain can I get what I need when I need it? The promise with the cloud is great, but the uncertainty has caused people to come up short and decide maybe it's better if I do it myself, versus utilizing an outside service."[6]

When discussing the issues associated with cloud security, a number of topics come to mind including, as quoted by Schmelzer:[7]

> . . . cloud availability; cloud security; erosion of data integrity; data replication and consistency issues; potential loss of privacy; lack of auditing and logging visibility; potential for regulatory violations; application sprawl and dependencies; inappropriate usage of services; difficulty in managing intra-cloud, inter-cloud, and cloud and non-cloud interactions and resources. And that's just the short list.

In the following sections, the results of a 2009 survey, we explore the key threats to cloud computing that have been discovered:[8]

- Abuse and nefarious use of cloud computing
- Insecure application programming interfaces
- Malicious insiders
- Shared technology vulnerabilities
- Data loss/leakage
- Account, service, and traffic hijacking
- Unknown risk profile

Abuse and Nefarious Use of Cloud Computing

Access to any specific cloud infrastructure is not limited to those with large financial resources. A hacker with a stolen credit card may be registered in a cloud environment next to a Fortune 500 financial services provider. Some cloud vendors may even allow free trial registration periods.

> PaaS providers have traditionally suffered most from this kind of attacks; however, recent evidence shows that hackers have begun to target IaaS vendors as well. Future areas of concern include password and key cracking, DDOS, launching dynamic attack points,

hosting malicious data, botnet command and control, building rainbow tables, and CAPTCHA solving farms.[9]

The solution? Vendors must increase the rigor and security in their registration process, specifically focusing on credit card fraud. Vigilance in monitoring for abuse is also paramount.

Insecure Application Programming Interfaces

In order to access cloud services, providers use software interfaces and APIs. Security of these functions is directly tied to security of the applications and data associated with them. Problem areas include "anonymous access and/or reusable tokens or passwords, clear-text authentication or transmission of content, inflexible access controls or improper authorizations, limited monitoring and logging capabilities, unknown service or API dependencies."[10] To deal with these issues, vendors must provide (and customers must demand) increased security in access controls and interface interaction via encryption.

Malicious Insiders

As mentioned earlier, the hacker next door may now have insider access to cloud infrastructures. Physical access also becomes an issue, as the third-party service providers may not desire to disclose their own physical security policies and procedures. Coupled with the possibility of international service providers, the problems increase exponentially. In order to resolve this, service level agreements (SLAs) must stipulate transparency in physical security measures. Customers must be vigilant in the evaluation and selection of service providers.

Shared Technology Vulnerabilities

The technologies developed and deployed in a cloud computing environment are not always designed to meet customer security expectations. For example, does the provider have the capability to prevent the data from one customer from rubbing up against data from another? In some database models, the data from multiple clients is co-mingled, using meta tags to differentiate it. No physical or even virtual segregation may be occurring. From a software perspective, the same issues occur; processing is distributed based on demand and availability. Flaws in hypervisors could allow one guest operating system to control or access information on another. Improvements in architecture and compartmentalization are needed to avoid cross-contamination. Periodic audits, scans, and compliance inspections are needed to support requirements of service agreements.

Data Loss/Leakage

When the organization does not have direct control of their data storage, they cannot regulate the protection mechanisms that keep it secure. As indicated in earlier issues, when the data from multiple customers is corralled into the same pen, so to speak, the potential for data loss or leakage increases exponentially. Strong authentication of authorized users of the data storage can help minimize the risks, but as long as the organization's data is stored outside its physical boundaries, risk will exist. A better understanding of how the vendor stores data and what protection mechanisms are present will serve to educate clients on vendor selection.

Account, Service, and Traffic Hijacking

While these attacks are certainly not new to information security, the communications channels they seek to intercept are. With cloud computing, additional communications to and from the cloud computing provider provide additional opportunities for a potential attacker to intercept. In the absence of strongly authenticated and encrypted communications, as in through a modern VPN, any communications made over the Internet to access a cloud computing provider must be assumed to be insecure. Vendors that provide proprietary connection applications, software, or hardware should be asked about the communications and security technologies that protect these channels. In the absence of acceptable encryption and authentication protections, the client should seriously consider their alternatives.

Unknown Risk Profile

The bottom line with cloud computing is that the client doesn't know. They don't know what hardware, software, applications, and data protection mechanisms are in place. They don't know how vigilant the cloud computing provider is in conducting risk assessments and mitigating their own risks. In a field where "don't know" can result in data loss and subsequently business loss, the organization may not be willing to invest in uncharted waters. Only through thoroughly investigating the cloud computing vendor's risk management and overall information security practices can the organization seek to minimize their own risks in engaging the cloud computing vendor. Wherever the client finds faults, the only recourse is to mandate certain protections in the service agreement.[11]

Other Security Issues in the Cloud

Other experts assert that, simply put, most of the security issues in the cloud are the exact same security issues associated with managing organizationally owned equipment, with one major drawback. When dealing with SaaS, the security issues center on access controls and password issues (weak credentials), communications protocol issues, and web-based application flaws.[12] PaaS has issues with the configuration of the applications provided, the implementation and deployment of SSL and permissions issues with cloud-stored data.[13] When using IaaS, the number one security issue is the security of the underlying operating system and services.[14]

So, what is the drawback to controlling these risks in cloud computing applications? The organization can't control any of this directly. As a leased service, the organization may or may not have any say in the implementation of security of the leased services. What the organization does have control over is the number one security tool in the cloud computing arena—the service agreement. As discussed in later sections of this chapter, the content of the service agreement will be the organizations primary method of auditing and assuring the security of the cloud-side leased services and their underlying components. Governing those components, their protection and use through these service agreements is the cornerstone of governance.

GOVERNANCE

Corporate governance begat IT Governance, which begat Information Security (InfoSec) Governance. Both the governance of the information technology uses of the organization and the governance of the information security program that secures the information stored, processed, and transmitted through the organization's IT infrastructure, and used by its entities for decision making, must address the governance of the latest IT evolution to face the field. Just as with many technologies deployed in the organization, it is the mandate of the organization's IT and InfoSec groups to collaborate and define the governance activities that will address the use of cloud computing in the enterprise.

When the concept of *cloud computing governance* is discussed, it gains the same duality faced by *computer security policy*. When one discusses policy, one must make the distinction between the managerial guidance document that is promoted to provide direction for all security efforts, and the configuration guidelines used by systems administrators to configure security on a particular computing device. In governance, one must now distinguish between the high-level strategic guidance and planning for all things security by senior management, and governance for the functioning of policies (the latter) a la service-oriented architectures (SOA). "Governance is a word that came to prominence with the adoption of SOA. In the world of SOA, it was divided into design-time governance (defining policies to Web services) and runtime governance (actually applying those policies to real-time traffic)."[15]

Governance is defined as:

> Setting clear expectations for the conduct (behaviors and actions) of the entity being governed, and directing, controlling, and strongly influencing the entity to achieve these expectations. It includes specifying a framework for decision making, with assigned decision rights and accountabilities, intended to consistently produce desired behaviors and actions. Governance relies on well-informed decision making and the assurance that such decisions are routinely enacted as intended. Governance is most effective when it is systemic, woven into the culture and fabric of organizational behaviors and actions. Governance actions create and sustain the connections among principles, policies, processes, products, people, and performance.[16]

For the purposes of this chapter, when the discussion is focused on strategic governance, it will be delineated from SOA-style governance via capitalization. Governance (capital G) is the board-level strategic planning and management of the security program, and in this case of security in and the use of cloud computing. The related perspective of governance (lower case g) is the SOA governance approach to imposing policies and monitoring services at the micro-level. In reality, this level of governance is more an aspect of *control*, which is a subset of management, which is, in turn, a subset of true governance.

> Governing for enterprise security means viewing adequate security as a non-negotiable requirement of being in business. If an organization's management—including boards of directors, senior executives and all managers—does not establish and reinforce the business need for

effective enterprise security, the organization's desired state of security will not be articulated, achieved, or sustained. To achieve a sustainable capability, organizations must make enterprise security the responsibility of leaders at a governance level, not of other organizational roles that lack the authority, accountability, and resources to act and enforce compliance.[17]

InfoSec Governance, as a subset of Information Technology Governance, is a management philosophy only recently coming into its own. InfoSec Governance provides strategic vision and guidance to the implementation of information security in the organization. With the increased focus and attention given to cloud computing, it is essential that the organization formally address the security and management issues associated with this innovation.

According to the Corporate Governance Task Force, an alliance of industry and government sectors, strategic oversight regarding information security [includes]:

- Understanding the criticality of information and information security to the organization
- Reviewing investment in information security for alignment with the organization strategy and risk profile
- Endorsing the development and implementation of a comprehensive information security program.
- Requiring regular reports from management on the program's adequacy and effectiveness[18]

In order for InfoSec Governance to be considered effective, the organization must:

Demonstrate a set of beliefs, behaviors, capabilities, and actions that consistently indicate that an organization is addressing security as a governance concern:

- Security is enacted at an enterprise level.
- Security is treated the same as any other business requirement.
- Security is considered during normal strategic and operational planning cycles.
- Security is integrated into enterprise functions and processes.
- All personnel who have access to enterprise networks understand their individual responsibilities with respect to protecting and preserving the organization's security condition[19]

IT Governance in the Cloud

Governance is the managerial obligation to:

- Ensure business value is recognized from IT-enabled business investments
- Establish a solid base for a defensible standard of due care
- Demonstrate due diligence to that defensible standard[20]

Key elements for good governance in risk and control (GRC) for cloud computing and the virtualization technologies that enable cloud computing include:

- Top-down engagement
- Clear roles and responsibilities
- Proactive—linked to business plan
- Business risk-based standard of care clearly articulated
- Clear methods for buy/build analysis with a complete cost model bought off by all stakeholders
- "Inspect what you Expect"
- Do not outsource what you could not manage anyway
- Match the IT model to the company culture[21]

The issues in securing (and governing) cloud computing use mirror those of any other IT and InfoSec governance issue: ensuring good security in protecting the access, transmission, and storage of data. Accomplishment of this in a cloud environment is through the use of legal documents mandating compliance with acceptable security standards through service-level agreements. The governance strategies that must be pursued by organizations wishing to participate in the benefits of cloud computing don't differ greatly from those that don't. The major difference is in the degree of vigilance one must assert over the only protection mechanisms available to the client—the service agreement.

Managing Service Agreements

The service agreement is a legal contract that guarantees the vendor will provide specified services for a specified rate, subject to certain conditions. It is the specification of conditions that adds value to the service beyond cost. The only recourses available to the client, should the vendor breach the service agreement, are litigation and discontinuance of service.

An SLA is an agreement to provide services between a service provider and a service consumer. This is usually done either as a standard element of a contract for services when it exists between organizations, or it may exist as a policy element or informal agreement between organizational units within a larger organization. Some may believe that all service contracts will contain SLA elements, but this is not always the case. Unless the service consumer has consciously negotiated the proposed levels of service articulated by the service provider, it is simply a contract for services. From an InfoSec perspective, any SLA should include details of exactly what levels of protection the service provider will deliver and maintain to warrant the confidentiality, integrity and availability of all information being held or transmitted.

When negotiating an SLA for cloud computing services a number of governance issues must be clearly identified, discussed, and negotiated. Only by ensuring the organization, its business functions, and its data protection are guaranteed can the organization safely engage in cloud computing.

The top issues in cloud computing service agreements that the governance committee should review are:

- Support for outages
- Assurance of data
- Incident response procedures
- Auditability of security
- Financial restitution for lost business
- Certification of trust

Outage concerns—if an organization's business is conducted purely through the cloud, what happens in a cloud outage? What are the liability issues associated with lost business, and lost revenues? Some of this can be addressed through service agreements, but most cloud vendors will prove unwilling to reimburse a cloud service customer for lost business in the event of an internal outage. External outages, resulting from natural disasters, regional power outages and the like, will continue to be dismissed as acts of God and thus covered only under service fees, if at all. Seldom will a vendor offer to reimburse lost business from these areas. However, loss due to internal failures, power issues, server crashes, networking issues, or even worse, a hacker, should specifically be addressed in any cloud computing service agreements, and both parties must agree on the restitution in the event of an outage. Recent discussions have identified these liability issues as one of the most detrimental to widespread adoption.[22]

IMPLEMENTING AND MAINTAINING GOVERNANCE FOR CLOUD COMPUTING

To establish an effective governance strategy for cloud computing, the organization must first select an implementation methodology. If the organization already has a governance structure in place for IT and InfoSec, it can move to the Extending IT Governance to the Cloud section of this chapter.

Implementing Governance as a New Concept

For the organization that has not previously implemented a governance structure, a number of preliminary functions must be handled before governance of the cloud can even be considered. First, a governance structure for IT and Information Security must be established. The following provides an excellent overview of IT and Information Security Governance, and can assist in setting up the governance structure. The key components of the implementation of a new governance structure are highlighted here.

Preliminary Tasks

Before completely investing in the governance process, a series of preliminary tasks should be performed. These tasks allow the organization to lay a solid foundation upon which to build a successful governance program.

Identify the Stakeholders   The first task is to identify those groups that will have a vested interest in the governance structure and who may be directly involved. These groups include:

- Executive management
- Business management and business process owners
- Chief information officer (CIO), IT management, and IT process owners
- IT audit
- Information Security, including risk and compliance.[23]

Define the Governance Board   Once the stakeholders are identified, those who should, and who are willing to, serve on a governance board should be identified. Once identified, their primary roles and responsibilities should be defined. According to ISACA, these roles include the following:

- **Board and executives**—Set direction for the program, ensure alignment with enterprise-wide governance and risk management, approve key program roles and define responsibilities, and give visible support and commitment. Sponsor, communicate, and promote the agreed-upon initiative.
- **Business management**—Provide appropriate stakeholders and champions to drive commitment and to support the program. Nominate key program roles and define and assign responsibilities.
- **IT management**—Ensure that the business and executives understand and appreciate the high-level objectives. Nominate key program roles and define and assign responsibilities. Nominate a person to drive the program in agreement with the business.
- **IT audit**—Agree on the role and reporting arrangements for audit participation. Ensure that an adequate level of audit participation is provided through the duration of the program.
- **[Information Security] risk and compliance**—Ensure an adequate level of participation through the duration of the program.[24]

Review the Key Success Factors   A key success factor, or critical success factor, is something that must go right for the operation to succeed. Absence of these factors can substantially decrease the probability of success in the venture. For IT (and InfoSec) governance, the key success factors are:

- **Top management investiture.** More than simply a memo from top management, executive management must demonstrate investiture in the governance structure by meeting and establishing the direction and purpose (mandate) for the governance function. They must demonstrate to the entire organization that they are dedicated to the process.
- **Understanding of the outcomes and objectives.** In addition to understanding the impetus of the governance function, all stakeholders in the process must understand *why* the governance is being done; the business, IT, and InfoSec objectives; and the desired governance outcomes.
- **Change management.** In order for any change to be effective and established as the new organizational culture, the projected changes to result from the governance effort must be clearly communicated and then enabled.

▪ **Customization of the governance framework to the organization.**
A careful adaptation of any governance framework is required to ensure it
meets the needs and ability of the organization. The tailoring of the practices
and procedures must be carefully effected to maximize compatibility.

▪ **Pick the low-hanging fruit.** The project should look for activities that
can be quickly implemented with clear benefits realized. Identify those
components of the governance project, like an executive briefing on
InfoSec issues in the cloud that can be easily and quickly performed,
with immediate results realized.[25]

Adopt a Governance Implementation Methodology

The following governance implementation methodology, taken from ISACA's
Implementing and Continually Improving IT Governance,[26] can be used to initiate
the governance function:

Phase 1: Initiate the Program: What are the drivers?   Phase 1 identifies
current change drivers and creates at executive management levels a desire to
change that is then expressed in an outline of a business case. Risks associated
with implementation of the IT governance program itself will be described in
the business case and managed throughout the life cycle. A change driver is an
internal or external event, condition or key issue that serves as a stimulus for
change. Events, trends (industry, market, or technical), performance shortfalls,
software implementations and even the goals of the enterprise can act as
change drivers.

Phase 2: Define Problems and Opportunities: Where are we now?   Phase
2 aligns IT objectives with business strategies and risks, and prioritizes the most
important IT goals and processes (including controls). COBIT provides a generic
mapping of business goals to IT goals to IT processes to help with the selection
of goals. Given the defined IT goals, critical processes are defined, managed,
and controlled to ensure successful outcomes.

Management needs to know its current capability and where deficiencies
may exist. This is achieved by a capability maturity model assessment of the as-
is status of the selected processes and controls.

Phase 3: Define the Road Map: Where do we want to be?   Phase 3 sets
a target for improvement followed by a gap analysis to identify potential
solutions. Some solutions will be quick wins and others more challenging,

long-term tasks. Priority should be given to projects that are easier to achieve and likely to give the greatest benefit. Longer-term tasks should be broken down into manageable pieces.

Phase 4: Plan the Program: What needs to be done?   Phase 4 plans feasible and practical solutions by defining projects supported by justifiable business cases, and developing a change plan for implementation. A well-developed business case will help ensure that the project's benefits are identified and monitored. Val IT provides an example template and guidance for preparation of a business case.

Phase 5: Execute the Plan: How do we get there?   Phase 5 provides for the implementation of the proposed solutions into day-to-day practices, and the establishment of measures and monitoring systems to ensure that business alignment is achieved and performance can be measured. Success requires engagement, awareness and communication, understanding and commitment of top management, and ownership by the affected business and IT process owners.

Phase 6: Realize Benefits: Did we get there?   Phase 6 focuses on sustainable transition of the improved management practices into normal business operations, and monitoring achievement of the improvement by measuring performance metrics and the expected benefits.

Phase 7: Review Effectiveness: How do we keep the momentum going?   Phase 7 reviews the overall success of the initiative, identifies further governance requirements, and reinforces the need for continual improvement.

While reporting is not mentioned explicitly in any of the phases, it is a continual thread through all of the phases and iterations.[27]

The ISACA Governance Methodology is illustrated in Exhibit 3.1.

Extending IT Governance to the Cloud

Once the organization has an established governance function, how can this be extended to cloud computing use? The answer is simply to apply the governance framework to the cloud computing decision.

Phase 1: Initiate the Program: What are the drivers?   During this phase, the IT (and InfoSec) Groups must thoroughly research the cloud computing

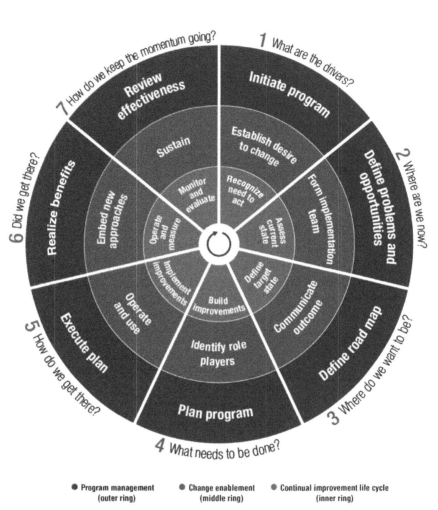

● Program management   ● Change enablement   ● Continual improvement life cycle
(outer ring)   (middle ring)   (inner ring)

EXHIBIT 3.1   The ISACA Governance Implementation and Continuous Improvement Methodology

Source: ISACA, www.isaca.org.

environment, including general advantages and disadvantages. The various stakeholders should be briefed on these items. The question of what drivers are forcing the organization to consider cloud computing must be evaluated.

Phase 2: Define Problems and Opportunities: Where are we now?   Here, the governance board determines if the adoption of cloud computing supports the current organizational business strategies and risks. If the determination is that cloud computing would become an important IT function, it is prioritized with other IT functions, projects, and proposals. The current organizational functions and their shortcomings must be determined in light of a potential cloud computing implementation. What problems will cloud computing resolve? What problems will cloud computing create? The latter question will require careful involvement of legal and regulatory council, to ensure the deployment of organizational data to be migrated to cloud computing will not create additional issues.

Phase 3: Define the Road Map: Where do we want to be?   The governance board must determine what strategic value will result from cloud computing implementation. What improvements in the organization will result from cloud computing adoption? The level of complexity, time frame for implementation, and challenges associated with cloud computing adoption are considered.

Phase 4: Plan the Program: What needs to be done?   During this phase, a cloud computing investigatory subgroup is appointed, consisting of IT, InfoSec, and business representatives, to evaluate cloud computing vendors and services more thoroughly. It is during this phase, where a complete risk assessment of cloud computing is conducted, given the service agreements from potential vendors. It is here, before any one vendor is selected, that the organization has the most pull in ensuring acceptable levels of protection of data to be stored on vendor systems, as well as in the level of security assessment and transparency that will be provided to systems leased to the organization. It is also here that the organization would expect the vendors to share information on their own security practices, including personnel and physical security functions.

Phase 5: Execute the Plan: How do we get there?   Once this phase is reached, the organization begins to deploy cloud computing. Closely monitoring the implementation, security and operation of business activities as cloud computing is deployed can serve to negate potential security issues. Throughout this process, the governance board must keep a watchful eye on issues arising from migration, comparing them to the negotiated service agreements, to determine compliance.

Phase 6: Realize Benefits: Did we get there?   Once the organization has completely implemented cloud computing, it must begin a performance measures (metrics) program to monitor and evaluate ongoing operations for Phase 7. The organization must determine at this stage: Did we meet our desired objectives and outcomes? Are we realizing the benefits we expected? Is continual use at this stage justified?

Phase 7: Review Effectiveness: How do we keep the momentum going? The maintenance and change phase of the cloud computing implementation is the most critical. On a regular basis the governance board should review the performance measures collected on cloud computing deployment, and make the ongoing decision to either continue cloud computing use or discontinue it, either with a particular vendor or in totality. The governance board has the continual responsibility to monitor and guide the future use of this technology, just as with any deployed technology. However, unlike most deployed technologies, the external trust issues between the organization and its cloud computing vendor creates a level of permanent discomfort that can never be fully resolved. Just as an investor carefully monitors his or her investment portfolio to ensure maximum return on the use of his or her monies, the organization must continually monitor the interaction between the employees using the cloud computing services and the third-party vendor providing them.

IN SUMMARY

While the benefits of cloud computing can be well worth the financial investments, the cost can extend well beyond the financial. Organizations must carefully weigh the risks of using cloud computing against perceived benefits. Only after a formal governance committee addresses these costs and benefits should cloud computing be considered. That said, the use of cloud computing can actually serve as a very successful risk management strategy in its own right. One of the formal risk management strategies an organization can implement is transference wherein the risk from some or all aspects of an operation is transferred to another entity. When implemented properly, it may be possible to shift risk to the entity providing the cloud service. The benefits associated with cloud computing are reminiscent of the consultant movement in the 1980s. Consultants Tom Peters and Bob Waterman are best known for their text *In Search of Excellence,*[28] in which they tout the lessons learned by excellent companies—those defined as extremely successful and leaders in their respective fields. One of the key idioms from the text was that excellent organizations focus on core competencies. That is, they do what they do best, and outsource that which they do not do well. Cloud computing can provide the organizations with another vehicle to accomplish this level of excellence, allowing the organization to focus on IP development, without having to build, maintain, and staff an entire data center or IT department outside their core skill sets.

However, the risks identified from governance concerns in cloud computing must be carefully assessed and accepted through some form of formal risk management strategy. The organization that simply accepts the extant risk can find itself losing all the benefits gained from cloud computing, and more.

NOTES

1. Gardner, D. 2010. Cloud Models and Managing Transition Risks Using Security Governance. IT Analysis. www.it-analysis.com/business/content.php?cid= 10905 (accessed July 27, 2010).
2. Williams, P. 2009. Governance in the Cloud. ComputerWeekly.com. www .computerweekly.com/blogs/it-governance/2009/11/governance-in-the-cloud .html (accessed July 27, 2010).
3. Ibid.
4. Ashford, W. 2009. IT Chiefs: Security is Biggest Threat to Cloud Computing. ComputerWeekly.com. www.computerweekly.com/Articles/2009/04/28/ 235821/IT-chiefs-Security-is-biggest-threat-to-cloud-computing.htm (accessed July 27, 2010).
5. Ashford, W. 2010. Is Your Data Secure in the Cloud? ComputerWeekly.com. www.computerweekly.com/Articles/2010/02/22/240380/is-your-data-secure-in-the-cloud.htm (accessed July 27, 2010).
6. Gardner, D. 2010. Cloud Models and Managing Transition Risks using Security Governance. IT Analysis. www.it-analysis.com/business/content.php?cid= 10905 (accessed July 27, 2010).
7. Schmelzer, R. 2009. Cloud Governance: Something Old, Something New, Something Borrowed . . . ZapThink. www.zapthink.com/2009/07/07/ cloud-governance-something-old-something-new-something-borrowed8230/ (accessed July 27, 2010).
8. CSA. 2010. Top Threats to Cloud Computing V1.0. Cloud Security Alliance. www.cloudsecurityalliance.org/topthreats/csathreats.v1.0.pdf (accessed July 27, 2010).
9. Ibid.
10. Ibid.

11. Ibid.
12. Cox, P. 2009b. How to Use Software as a Service Securely. SearchCloud Computing.com. http://searchcloudcomputing.techtarget.com/tip/0,289 483,sid201_gci1376180,00.html (accessed February 27, 2010).
13. Cox, P. 2009a. How to Use Platform as a Service Securely. SearchCloud Computing.com. http://searchcloudcomputing.techtarget.com/tip/0,289483, sid201_gci1376654,00.html (accessed February 27, 2010).
14. Cox, P. 2009c. Securing IaaS Operating Systems Vulnerabilities. SearchCloud Computing.com. http://searchcloudcomputing.techtarget.com/tip/0,289483, sid201_gci1377268,00.html (accessed February 27, 2010).
15. O'Neill, M. 2009. Connecting to the Cloud, Part 3: Cloud Governance and Security. IBM Technical Library. www.ibm.com/developerworks/xml/library/x-cloudpt3/ (accessed July 27, 2010).
16. Allen, J. 2005. Governing for Enterprise Security: Networked Systems Survivability Program. Technical Note: CMU/SEI-2005-TN-023. www.sei.cmu.edu/library/abstracts/reports/05tn023.cfm (accessed August 1, 2010).
17. Ibid.
18. ITGI. 2006. Information Security Governance: Guidance for Boards of Directors and Executive Management, 2nd edition. IT Governance Institute. www.isaca.org/Knowledge-Center/Research/ResearchDeliverables/Pages/Information-Security-Governance-Guidance-for-Boards-of-Directors-and-Executive-Management-2nd-Edition.aspx (accessed June 15, 2010).
19. Allen, J. 2005. Governing for Enterprise Security: Networked Systems Survivability Program. Technical Note: CMU/SEI-2005-TN-023. www.sei.cmu.edu/library/abstracts/reports/05tn023.cfm (accessed August 1, 2010).
20. Spokes, J., and K. Worstell. 2009. Governance in Cloud and Virtualized Environments. ISACA Webcast. www.brighttalk.com/webcast/4078 (accessed August 10, 2010).
21. Ibid.
22. Smith, L. 2010. Enterprise Adoption of the Public Cloud Hinges on Liability Policies. SearchCIO. http://itknowledgeexchange.techtarget.com/total-cio/enterprise-adoption-of-the-public-cloud-hinges-on-liability-policies/?track=NL-964&ad=778405&asrc=EM_NLN_12190729&uid=9679238 (accessed August 10, 2010).
23. ISACA, 2009. Implementing and Continually Improving IT Governance. www.isaca.org/Knowledge-Center/cobit/Documents/Implement-cont-improve-it-gov-17aNov09.pdf?Token=077A9B00-73A5-450F-B56E-DCB891851B76 (accessed August 13, 2010).
24. Ibid.
25. Ibid.
26. Ibid.
27. Ibid.

28. Peters, T. J., & R. H. Waterman. 1982. *In Search of Excellence: Lessons from America's Best-Run Companies.* New York: Harper & Row.

REFERENCES

Gartner Group. 2010. Gartner Hype Cycle. www.gartner.com/technology/research/methodologies/hype-cycle.jsp (accessed August 13, 2010).

Lageschulte, P., and P. Rapp. 2009. Cloud Computing: Business Benefits with Security, Governance and Assurance Perspectives. ISACA Webcast. Viewed 8/5/2010 from http://mediazone.brighttalk.com/comm/ISACA/6e36e06dcd-17044-733-18415

Wikipedia. Service Level Agreement. 2004. http://en.wikipedia.org/wiki/Service_level_agreement (accessed August 10, 2010)

CHAPTER FOUR

System and Infrastructure Lifecycle Management for the Cloud

Steve Riley*

I N THIS CHAPTER, we examine how traditional lifecycle management techniques can be applied to cloud deployments. We consider how traditional lifecycle management processes require some adaptation for the cloud and discuss the notion of *handoff*—where a customer's own processes end and a provider's processes begin. We suggest how you can verify that your lifecycle controls are indeed practical and being followed. And we briefly touch on the distinct challenges that cross-cloud deployments present. First, though, we need to introduce (or perhaps reinforce) the notion of *tradeoffs*.

EVERY DECISION INVOLVES MAKING A TRADEOFF

You might not realize it, but you make tradeoffs every single day of your life. In many cases, these are security tradeoffs that we fail to realize have any relation to security or the notion of exchanging one thing for another. For example,

* The author wishes to convey his gratitude to Chad Woolf and Max Ramsay for their significant contributions, and to Stephen Schmidt for his valuable input.

consider bulletproof vests. They have a very valuable security function: They save you from getting killed by gunshots. So why didn't you put one on before you walked out of your house this morning? The likelihood of you getting shot is greater than zero percent, wouldn't you agree? So shouldn't you take every precaution possible to minimize that likelihood even more?

The reason you don't wear a bulletproof vest every day is because you realize, intrinsically, that while stray bullets strike victims with some regularity, the likelihood of any one particular bullet claiming you as its victim is vanishingly small. Plus, bulletproof vests are heavy, uncomfortable, hot, and make for poor fashion. So, in this instance you're deciding to forego the obvious disadvantages of vest encumbrance, and accepting the very small risk of taking a bullet.[1]

The same principle of choosing among tradeoffs applies to choosing cloud deployments and accepting the risks that come with your choice. Ultimately, it means understanding your own comfort level with transferring certain security, control, and management responsibilities to your provider. With classic on-premise deployments you have complete control over the infrastructure you build, the platforms you deploy, the applications you run, and the data you create. In the cloud, you transition control of some of these elements to your provider—and the elements you transfer depend on how that provider has built their services.

One way to visualize this is to note how responsibilities for control change as you move from on-premise deployments to providers of infrastructure services, platform services, and software services. See Exhibit 4.1.

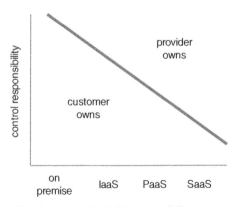

EXHIBIT 4.1   Cloud Deployment Model Responsibility

As you evaluate controls associated with cloud deployments, where the handoff happens depends on where in the stack your provider specializes:

- Infrastructure providers take care of physical controls: buildings, network cables, compute and storage hardware, and the software that manages the infrastructure; you retain control of operating systems, applications, and data.
- Platform providers build on top of infrastructure providers by taking care of operating systems and often providing a limited set of development environments; you retain control of applications and data.
- Software providers build on top of application providers by offering fully hosted software suites; you retain control only of the data.

Generally, the needs of your business and any particular applicable regulatory frameworks will help you determine which model suits you best. It could very well be that you'll employ different providers for different projects. As any good consultant would say, "It depends."

Example: Business Continuity/Disaster Recovery

Most infrastructure lifecycle management plans incorporate procedures for ensuring business continuity and recovering from disasters. When an organization relies entirely on in-house IT, Business Continuity/Disaster Recovery (BC/DR) can consume a lot of resources, both human and technical. Cloud computing offloads your BC/DR to the extent that the provider takes it on; the BC/DR offload curve follows the diagram shown in Exhibit 4.1.

If, for instance, you're working mostly with an IaaS provider, you can implement a BC/DR plan that requires minimal resources by taking advantage of that provider's features such as multiple geographic regions, automatic data replication, performance monitoring, and automatic failover. The features are there not only for the provider to rely on but also for you to build systems with those features in mind.

If you're working with an SaaS provider, then there isn't much BC/DR planning you need to do yourself. You should, however, ask for and receive from your provider a thorough explanation of their BC/DR plans to ensure that your own business requirements will be met. Request from your SaaS provider documentation that explains their control objectives and how they have planned for business continuity. In the case of SaaS-level clouds, especially, provider business continuity has a direct bearing on the business continuity of their customers. (We discuss this in greater detail in the verification section of this chapter.)

WHAT ABOUT POLICY AND PROCESS COLLISIONS?

One of the largest areas of concern many people tend to overlook is that cloud providers have their own policies, which are most likely very different from your own. Your policies are based on your business needs and regulatory concerns. The cloud provider's policies are largely based on providing services to a large set of customers in a consistent manner. This difference will often lead to tensions that breed angst for customers and frustration for cloud providers.

For instance, say that you have a policy requiring certain training for people with trusted access to sensitive data—this training (ideally refreshed regularly) reminds your staff of your specific policies and processes for dealing with that data. Furthermore, according to the policy, you require contractors to follow the same procedures when they manage applications or infrastructure for you that processes or stores that data. One of your business units decides to host some new application with a cloud provider. It's very likely that the cloud provider won't agree to comply with your standards for managing that data simply because their business is to provide consistent service to a large number of customers. So then, what do you do?

You're now faced with some tough decisions:

- Do you try to force with the cloud provider to adopt your standards? This likely won't work unless you have enough scale to catch their attention.
- Do you force the business unit to choose a traditional vendor? Another difficult decision because your executives are all looking for the promised savings and efficiencies that cloud computing promises.
- Do you abandon your standards simply because they are not "*cloud friendly*"? We're sure your auditors wouldn't like that too much.

The path that's left is to take a hard look at your requirements and figure out why they've grown to the extent they have over the years. Evaluate them against what you really need versus what's grown over time to address some shortcomings in the environments in which you've traditionally been working. Examine what the cloud provider offers in terms of features that will help you achieve your business goals. Work with your cloud vendor to understand some of the details they will only convey under a non-disclosure agreement and see what compromises might be achievable. Work with your regulator/ auditor to incorporate their concerns. Finally, evaluate the gap and help the business unit and executives understand the business risk they are accepting by moving forward.

Sometimes, you'll realize that you're now positioned in a stronger, less risky position than that of traditional environments. Sometimes you'll find an acceptable level of risk. Sometimes you'll find the risk is too high and you will need to seek an alternate solution that meets your critical requirements. Either way, your organization can move forward with buy-in from key stakeholders.

THE SYSTEM AND MANAGEMENT LIFECYCLE ONION

Given the layered models around which cloud computing has coalesced, we present the system and infrastructure management lifecycle onion. Why an onion, rather than something more pleasingly fragrant? Well, the farther up the cloud service stack you go, the fewer layers you need to manage yourself. You can peel away and discard the layers that don't matter to you and concentrate on those that do. An illustration should help (see Exhibit 4.2):

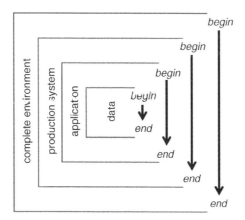

EXHIBIT 4.2 Cloud Onion Layers

Within each layer, you'll iterate through a series of steps and evaluate the controls that are or should be in place. Classic lifecycle steps follow this pattern:

- Plan
- Prototype
- Deploy
- Maintain
- Decommission

Every data object, every application, every system running an application, and every complete environment has a beginning, an existence, and an end. Lifecycle management controls should govern every step at every layer. When evaluating which controls matter, it's important to keep a number of points in mind:

- Does this control mitigate a known risk?
- What's the likelihood of that risk actually happening?
- What's the exposure if the risk is realized?
- Is the cost of implementing the control proportional to the cost of exposure?
- What is the fallout if you ignore the risk?
- What is the backup or response mechanism if the control itself fails?
- Have you properly anticipated, evaluated, and ranked unknown risks?

MAPPING CONTROL METHODOLOGIES ONTO THE CLOUD

Fortunately, much of the grunt work involved in determining applicable controls and measuring their effectiveness has already been done by various organizations that enjoy that kind of thing. Two of the more common lifecycle methodologies are COBIT and ITIL. While these can be adjusted to map to cloud deployments, the overarching drive behind these methodologies is about managing components and the service delivery aspects associated with those components. In the cloud these components become abstract concepts; the farther up the cloud service stack you go, the more abstract they become. When an infrastructure provider builds an offering and guarantees it with a defined service level agreement (SLA), the elements of traditional lifecycle frameworks around SLAs evaporate: you work within the provider's SLA.

Lifecycle management in the cloud shifts from managing component reliability to managing service reliability.

One way of thinking about this is to anticipate and then measure the expected user experience. Business units should have a good idea of the performance requirements of their applications at various times throughout the day; for example, if you're auditing whether an application's performance matches expectations, you'll need to conduct tests not only under minimal and peak workloads (the typical things you'd test) but also tests that exercise your provider's ability to rapidly scale up and down. You need to understand, before production time, how you (and your customers) will experience the scaling process.[2] Your tests will reveal whether the provider's underlying infrastructure properly scales when the application makes demands that it do so; there's no need to audit the actual infrastructure components themselves. The automated on-demand elasticity that intrinsically defines *cloud* removes much of the manual process-oriented and component-based lifecycle management tasks that traditional in-house IT deployments must endure.

Organizations that establish a good discipline for deploying to the cloud will often be able to rely on the provider's management tools for measuring service reliability. Third parties have created products that build on top of these capabilities to add more granular levels of configuration and control. And some firms now offer independent near-real-time global performance monitoring of multiple cloud providers. Organizations with poor internal discipline will find that the cloud at first magnifies the lack of control: its pay-as-you-go model practically cries out for business units to circumvent IT governance choke points. Eventually, cloud-based deployments will become the norm and in-house deployments will require exceptions. Fortunately, updated versions of the frameworks will address this fundamental shift in the management and governance of IT projects. For now, though, let's briefly examine three resources.

Information Technology Infrastructure Library

Some of Information Technology Infrastructure Library's (ITIL's) elements map to cloud deployments; in almost all cases, though, there will be a certain amount of translation required—translation from ITIL's focus on process to the cloud's foundations in automation:

- Service Portfolio Management (to map business and application requirements onto the cloud provider's offerings)

- Service Level Management (to ensure the provider's metrics align to the business requirements)
- Demand and Capacity Management (with the understanding that cloud resources are metered and can scale on-demand automatically)
- Financial Management (the meter's rate can change depending on the billing options chosen and the time of day)
- Change Control (using the cloud provider's built-in features for replicating a production environment, conducting test and QA, and then transitioning to the updated system—probably the biggest change from ITIL's rigid and time-consuming process)
- Service Validation and Testing (to ensure the service levels remain as expected)

Control Objectives for Information and Related Technology

Similarly, the Control OBjectives for Information and related Technology (COBIT) framework can be abbreviated when applying it to the cloud. The most important ones to focus on are those in the Deliver and Support domain. Many of the processes in the other domains move outside your scope of responsibility: for example, those governing physical hardware procurement and maintenance. Depending on where in the cloud service stack your provider falls, additional processes may move beyond your scope, too. If you're deploying a project on an SaaS provider, there's not much you need to do with regard to change and configuration management.

It's a good idea to inquire of your provider what their control objectives are and how they're measured; providers unwilling to share this information probably aren't worthy of your businesses. Providers who do share this information make it much easier for you to incorporate their governance framework into yours so that, by inclusion, you can document a complete framework for each phase of the management lifecycle.

COBIT is undergoing a major revision; ISACA is currently at work on version 5. New governance process models will be overlaid on the existing domains and additional domains will be incorporated. Cloud computing will affect some of the process models in important ways.

- **Resource Management.** Thoughtful and effective cloud computing deployments reduce the resource management burden typically required for in-house IT. Largely, this requires adopting a new mindset, moving away from internally-focused infrastructure management and toward a view that primarily considers how best to match resources to demand, to maximize business value. One interesting technical note is that the shift to cloud computing will most likely require organizations to increase the amount of network bandwidth over what they're using now.

- **Risk Management.** It's probably obvious by now, but just to make sure you understand: deploying to the cloud essentially means you're outsourcing some elements of your risk management to your provider. In many cases, this can result in an overall improvement: providers have dedicated risk management staff and are successful businesses largely because they know they simply have to get this aspect done right. Your risk management plan will include elements of your provider's plan, especially those related to availability, durability, business continuity/disaster recovery, outages, and remedies. With proper architectures, cloud deployments that make maximum use of the provider's redundancy features can be made virtually outage-free; this requires a thorough understanding of the provider's technical features and how to build your systems to take advantage of them. Part of your risk management plan should include an evaluation of your provider's procedures for handling data breaches and responding to requests from government agencies. Also, don't forget to examine your provider's long-term viability and note any mechanisms they provide for taking all your data and going someplace else, should you ever need to do that.

- **Performance Measurement.** Many of COBIT's domains help IT departments manage and report their achievement performance to the business. Governance goals regarding performance will differ significantly in the cloud because many of the usual troublesome suspects—hardware delays, resource utilization, and so on—are no longer issues that affect project timelines.

National Institute of Standards and Technology

National Institute of Standards and Technology (NIST) Special Publication 800-37,[3] *Guide for Applying the Risk Management Framework to Federal Information Systems,* calls special attention to how cloud computing affects traditional approaches to managing information system boundaries and lifecycles:

> Changes to current information technologies and computing paradigms add complications to the traditional tasks of establishing information system boundaries and protecting the missions and business processes supported by organizational information systems. In

particular, net-centric architectures (e.g., service-oriented architectures [SOAs], cloud computing) introduce two important concepts: (i) *dynamic subsystems*; and (ii) *external subsystems*. While the concepts of dynamic subsystems and external subsystems are not new, the pervasiveness and frequency of their invocation in net-centric architectures can present organizations with significant new challenges.

Section 2.3.3 of the publication (the above paragraph is its introduction) is important reading for anyone tasked with auditing cloud lifecycle management. It will help you understand how cloud computing alters the usual thinking around control and responsibility boundaries.

Cloud Security Alliance

The Cloud Security Alliance (CSA) has released a controls matrix[4] tailored for cloud computing customers and providers:

> The Cloud Security Alliance Controls Matrix (CM) is specifically designed to provide fundamental security principles to guide cloud vendors and to assist prospective cloud customers in assessing the overall security risk of a cloud provider. The CSA CM provides a controls framework that gives detailed understanding of security concepts and principles that are aligned to the Cloud Security Alliance guidance in 13 domains. The foundations of the Cloud Security Alliance Controls Matrix rest on its customized relationship to other industry-accepted security standards, regulations, and controls frameworks such as the HITRUST CSF, ISO 27001/27002, ISACA COBIT, PCI, and NIST, and will augment or provide internal control direction for SAS 70 or SSAE 16 attestations provided by cloud providers. As a framework, the CSA CM provides organizations with the needed structure, detail and clarity relating to information security tailored to the cloud industry. The CSA CM strengthens existing information security control environments by emphasizing business information security control requirements, reduces and identifies consistent security threats and vulnerabilities in the cloud, provides standardized security and operational risk management, and seeks to normalize security expectations, cloud taxonomy and terminology, and security measures implemented in the cloud.

The CSA's matrix is a decent starting point for developing your own controls. Keep in mind, though, that even here there's no one-size-fits-all list.

For example, the CSA control matrix assigns patch management tasks to cloud providers but not to customers. If you're using an SaaS provider, that's true. If you've deployed an application to some virtual machines at an IaaS provider, you're responsible for keeping the operating systems in your virtual machines patched. The provider will patch the underlying host operating system but has no visibility into the state of the virtual machines you've provisioned.

VERIFYING YOUR LIFECYCLE MANAGEMENT

Understanding, documenting, and verifying that your controls are operating effectively is a complex task. Depending on the nature of the deployment, new risks are introduced and ownership of the controls will shift; both of these changes require more and/or new types of controls. This section addresses how to validate that your control environment is effective while leveraging cloud solutions.

Always Start with Compliance Governance

Regardless of how or where your IT is deployed, you must have adequate governance and control over your entire environment. It's the responsibility of every enterprise to understand your compliance objectives and requirements (from relevant sources), establish a control environment that meets those objectives and requirements, and then validate that your control environment is effective to the appropriate level.

Cloud deployment does not reduce the need to govern your compliance in the slightest. It's common for control owners to assume that moving IT into the cloud will in some way reduce the need to establish or validate that controls are operating effectively. This is incorrect: governance over the control environment is more important since you lose some granular control over some aspects of your environment. Although some of the responsibility to operate controls may be outsourced, you as the owner of the IT environment must ensure the proper controls are in place all along the IT chain. The cloud may in fact require additional or different types of controls and will somewhat complicate your compliance environment. The good news is that although compliance management complexity increases as risk points are introduced, the efforts necessary to operate the controls may decrease depending on your cloud deployment type and extent. This is generally true only assuming the cloud provider can meet your control needs.

Earlier we discussed ways in which common governance frameworks can be adjusted to better align with cloud computing. In this section, we address how distributing your IT into the cloud may impact your control environment and how you can get comfortable with the unique controls managed by external entities (the cloud providers).

Verification Method

Classical control validation frameworks follow a standard model:

- Understand your environment and document your compliance requirements and risk.
- Design and implement control objectives to mitigate those risks.
- Verify that the controls are in place and operating effectively by testing them.

When you deploy into the cloud, your environment changes, and so must your risk profile and controls. This is the source of much of the anxiety around moving to the cloud. Because organizations might not fully understand how their environment is affected by the move, putting anything on the cloud seems terrifying. But for our purposes, we assume this task can realistically be performed given the guidance in the previous section that peeled apart the lifecycle onion.

With a complete understanding of the environment and an inventory of added risks, you can now design controls that fit your new cloud deployed environment. This will take some creativity, as standards around this are not yet formalized and universally adopted. While standards can help get you started, they can't predict each and every possible risk faced by every organization; ultimately, you know your own risk tolerance best. The key is to properly define the objectives of the controls and then move to the activities that need to be performed regardless of who should perform them.

The focus of the control design analysis should be on the chain of custody of all data and transmissions. There are two elements to this: connection points and storage.

1. **Connection points.** What would normally be transmitted via an internal private network will now be transmitted over the Internet, requiring secure transfer methods (typically SSL/TLS). Another example might be connections to and from a cloud database or application. Each connection

should be evaluated (secure or not) as to what exposure it brings and to determine if a control needs to be put in place.

2. **Storage state.** Considering where the data is located and what kind of data is stored, you might require additional protection (such as encryption) for sensitive or otherwise critical information. Recovery and redundancy factors may also apply.

Once your control design is complete and in place, you can test it. Begin by determining which controls you own and which your cloud vendor will own. This should be done independently of whether or not you have the visibility and/or the technical capability of monitoring the controls.

Next, determine what you're capable of verifying (we won't cover here *how* to verify your own controls, as we assume you already possess this skill). Verifying the controls owned by you and your organization is straightforward because they're transparent to you. Verifying the controls owned by someone else will take some work because you have reduced transparency into your cloud vendor's control environment. You must either obtain documentation or work directly with your cloud providers to obtain verification of the acceptable controls in place for those controls you don't own. Determine what you can verify, how they might be verified, and what you would like to see from the vendor in the way of external certifications or, better still, the technical ability to implement controls over your own cloud-based environment.

Finally, perform the actual verification. During your own compliance activities you'll need to verify the operating effectiveness of all the controls you have identified. There are a few methods of verification of cloud controls.

- **Direct management.** The cloud vendor may provide you the ability to encrypt data or secure transfers. This is ideal since if you control it directly, you only need verification of general IT controls from the cloud provider. Other than that, you can implement controls as you see fit and as far as the cloud provider gives you granular control.
- **Control attestations.** Documents like a SAS 70 or SSAE 16 Type II reports are very useful for verifying controls on a granular level. These reports document specific controls and the findings of an independent auditor hired to test the operating effectiveness of those controls. This is a highly effective verification method because if the control objectives align with the controls you require, a third party will have attested the effectiveness of those particular controls. Reliance on SAS 70 or SSAE 16 reports is also generally permitted by external auditors and other

external certifying bodies. One item to note is that the cloud provider selects the controls to document for the report, allowing them to omit or not state controls with which they don't comply. If you require specific controls you should work with your cloud provider to bring those into the scope of the SAS 70 or SSAE 16 review.

- **Standards certifications.** Standards such as ISO 27001 are appealing because they prescribe an entire suite of control objectives (usually following those listed in ISO 27002). To get certified, a cloud provider must materially comply with the entire standard. The advantage here is that you can compare the effectiveness of one provider against another and even against your own in-house controls. The caveat—and yes, there is one—is that to be certified means you're *materially* compliant, not necessarily *actually* compliant with all elements of the standard. Certifiers have the discretion of determining the materiality of non-compliance of certain items and may award a certification if they believe the provider has a process in place to address the gaps. Be aware that your cloud provider may be ISO-certified but may also be working on a few elements of the standard and not actually performing a control you're expecting. It's best to work directly with the cloud provider to get assurance over the specific controls you require.

- **Right to audit.** With the increasing acceptance of SAS 70 Type II, SSAE 16 Type II, and ISO 27001/27002 certifications, individual *right-to-audit* clauses will become less common. Because these certifications are granted by firms who specialize in on-site auditing, they are effective substitutes for your own in-person inspections. Arranging your own on-site audit may be logistically difficult and won't materially add to your ability to verify anything other than what's already included in the provider's certification documents. Consider also that a provider who routinely permits many on-site inspections actually *introduces* risk to the provider's other customers. Each time a facility is opened for inspection, risk to every customer of that facility increases. While it might give you some degree of satisfaction to conduct your own on-site audit, think about how you would feel if the provider freely opened their facility to anyone and everyone who wanted to poke around?

Illustrative Example

Let's look at an example of an organization using a cloud-based data storage service to house some important enterprise data. The cloud service gives us full control of the data (they don't manage the data with any application), and they provide some encryption mechanisms to protect the data when stored. Following the verification model described above, we would:

1. **Understand our environment.** We need to understand and document the bounds of this service. In this case those bounds are the particular data set to be stored in the cloud and the connection points to and from the data. Because our example involves no applications and no operating systems, note that we can peel away most of the layers of the lifecycle onion and concentrate on only the innermost part. We also determine that the data stored here is somewhat critical data. No other systems or processing are affected.

2. **Design controls.** We determine the following controls are needed:
   a. Because this is critical data, we need encryption on the device itself.
   b. Authentication into the general computing environment should be enforced.
   c. Data access should be controlled on a granular level.
   d. All connections to that data should be secure.
   e. The hardware lifecycle should be well controlled, requiring adequate destruction of media when the hard drives are cycled.
   f. Let's also assume you're in an industry with mandatory requirements around degaussing all hard drives before they are decommissioned.

3. **Verify controls are operating.** In this case, we would consider the service and determine if we can control any of these items. For this scenario, we determine the following:
   a. The cloud provider provides an encryption service controlled by the customers. We own this and include it in our own control management framework.
   b. Logical access to the cloud storage environment in this case is managed through our own logical access path. We own this and verify no other data-plane access mechanism is possible. We understand that the provider uses a separate control plane to manage the service. We check what their SAS 70 or SSAE 16 report has to say about managing control plane access. If the audit is a Type II report (where the auditors have verified the control is operating effectively) we can rely on this control and add it to our control framework as being managed by an outside party.
   c. We discover that granular data access is not possible with this service. We may need a compensating control and enhance the logical access to the storage environment.

    d. We realize this isn't necessarily secure, so we contact the cloud provider to request encrypted session capability. The provider offers this as a service in conjunction with our data storage, so we buy that secure connection service and validate the sessions are encrypted by conducting some internal testing.

    e. Our provider is in complete control of the hardware lifecycle. We check their SAS 70 or SSAE 16 audit report and notice this is a control documented there. And again, if the SAS 70 or SSAE 16 audit is a Type II report, we can rely on this control and add it to our control framework as being managed by an outside party.

    f. There is no SAS 70 or SSAE 16 control about media sanitization. At this point we would need to reach out to the cloud provider to see if they perform this, and if we can verify it. Depending on their response, we might request they immediately start this process in a way that we can verify it (SAS 70, SSAE 16 or right to audit) or move off the platform if the requirement is mandatory.

This is a simple example, but as you can see the analysis can get complex as your cloud footprint expands.

 ## RISK TOLERANCE

One concept to note here is the notion of *risk tolerance.* When you deploy to the cloud you won't achieve the same kind of granularity and control of your environment you're accustomed to with traditional in-house IT infrastructure. Additionally, because all control frameworks aren't equally managed, you might need to adjust what you're willing to accept as verification evidence. Are you comfortable with a cloud provider's sales representative telling you they have the controls in place? Is a general industry certification acceptable? Do you require a specific control documented on a SAS 70 or SSAE 16 report and tested by an external auditor? (Remember that only Type II reports describe the opinions of an external auditor and the results of their tests.)

    You'll need to evaluate—and possibly alter—your risk tolerance as you better understand the visibility of controls, the strength of your verification method, and the details of evidence made available by the cloud providers. You might need to implement compensating controls if your risks exceed your comfort level. All cloud customers should make this evaluation of risk, controls, visibility, and verification capability and evaluate their risk tolerance when needed. An evaluation should be made at regular intervals (given the pace of change in this market), and in response to an event, such as a change in the IT environment or when internal/external events occur.

SPECIAL CONSIDERATIONS FOR CROSS-CLOUD DEPLOYMENTS

A truly innovative organization can even run intensive information processing environments across multiple public cloud providers at every cloud service level. As you can imagine, when the output of a workload from the IaaS-level process moves into the PaaS-level process, the customer loses control over the lifecycle components of the infrastructure elements; likewise, when the PaaS-level output moves into the SaaS-level process, the customer loses even more control over the lifecycle components of the application elements. While this isn't intrinsically problematic, it does mean that the remaining lifecycle controls available through the full processing chain—namely, those associated with the data—become most critical. How so? Let's consider an example.

Suppose that the customer's IaaS-level environment includes data volume encryption. If the entire environment were completely contained in the IaaS level, controls around data end-of-life can be very easy: simply delete the encryption key (and ensure that no other copies might be lying around someplace). That's all there is to it. Without the encryption key, the data volume is useless to a would-be attacker.

However, in the case above, that data has to move out of the encrypted volume at the IaaS level into an application running at the PaaS provider. Now it isn't enough simply to rely on key destruction; the application itself must be designed to accept incoming encrypted traffic, decrypt it only when necessary, and then re-encrypt it for storage. Remember, though, there's one final step: depositing the data with the SaaS-level provider. Here, the customer's choices are limited to whatever the SaaS provider is capable of accepting. Furthermore, when the data reaches its end of life, the customer must work closely with the SaaS provider to receive assurance that the data is truly destroyed.

Remember that the web of complexity increases as you employ multiple providers and multiple types of cloud services. You'll need to verify all controls, but each provider has a different control environment, is compliant with different standards and may have different management styles with variable risk tolerances. It's generally difficult to perform direct comparisons between providers who specialize at different cloud service levels because the nature of what they are providing is so diverse. That's why it's up to you, the customer, to understand their requirements and independently verify that your control objectives are being met regardless of the mechanisms in which each provider's services are delivered to you.

The cloud value proposition is strong for not only enterprises from every industry but also for certain cloud providers themselves. It's becoming more common that an SaaS provider will use a PaaS or an IaaS to deliver their software to your organization. Cloud providers are comfortable using cloud services because they understand the model already and are natural cloud advocates. But this makes uniform auditing and verification even more complex because you'll have to deal with dispersed control ownership plus compounded control reliance. Again, you need to understand your environment even among this complexity so that you can design and verify controls accordingly.

To follow this example to its ideal conclusion requires a fundamental change in the way information is protected. Protection must revolve around the thing that's most important: the actual data itself. The industry is making strides toward standard methods for data objects to express their own lifecycle policies; we support these efforts and encourage widespread adoption.

THE CLOUD PROVIDER'S PERSPECTIVE

From a cloud provider's standpoint, it's imperative to establish a control environment that will meet the requirements of their customers. This can be challenging since the customers have extremely diverse requirements that can't all be anticipated. Typically a provider will choose a smaller set of controls that are broadly applicable to many customers, which allows the provider to implement a very high level of control strength and verification capability. There's no getting around the fact that a cloud environment must be as good as, or in most cases better than what the customers themselves require. It's impossible to anticipate or meet all these requirements, but a cloud provider can obtain stringent certifications that often satisfy the majority of the verification requirement of its customers.

Another layer of complexity is introduced as cloud providers manage the challenge of juggling customer requirements with their own. Under the burden of increasing requirement complexity, cloud providers are compelled to maintain a disciplined compliance framework and unified control set, employing a method to meet multiple requirements with a common set of testing and verification activities—testing once for multiple objectives, for example.

One more concept to consider is the notion that a thorough and public documentation of a provider's control environment can introduce *more* risk for the entire base of customers. If a provider describes all controls explicitly, and announces the frequency of audits, how might an attacker make use of this knowledge? If a provider allows multiple customers to walk through data centers, potential attackers can memorize locations of cameras, count the number of guards, and observe shift rotation behaviors. Even well-meaning customers can trip and fall into racks. If too many people know the details of how a provider manages its security, this can introduce additional potential avenues of external attack. So providers must seriously consider the visibility balance to provide customers with the information they need without exposing the company and the customer base to an unacceptable level of risk. Sometimes, a little obscurity can be good for everyone.

Questions That Matter

It's typical for customers to provide prospective cloud providers with long questionnaires asking about security practices and techniques. While at first this idea appears to be appropriate due diligence, keep in mind that cloud providers offer the same suites of products to all their customers. As cloud computing grows in popularity and maturity, the capabilities of every provider will increase; all customers benefit from new products and features.

Here are a few examples of common questions that today are more historical artifacts than viable security controls.

- *Does the provider regularly back up all data to tape and store it offsite?* Mature cloud storage services are built to be fundamentally highly reliable. Usually, this is achieved by making multiple copies of every object and storing these copies across geographically separate physical locations. Cloud-based storage services are designed in such a way to drive the likelihood of data loss to near zero percent. Offsite tape backups are unnecessary because the very nature of the service includes the notion of multi-site copies of data objects that are all live and available.
- *Will the provider implement feature X or product Y in their data centers?* It's very rare for a provider to alter or amend their products for individual customers. To do so would dramatically increase the provider's costs and would dampen the economic value proposition. It would also increase the security burden on the provider: managing multiple sets of control objectives introduces additional risk because there are greater opportunities

for configuration mistakes to appear. One option to explore would be what mechanisms the provider offers for connecting from their cloud to product Y if you choose to locate that in your own data center or in a colocation facility.

- *How many people have access to the provider's facilities? How many people have root or administrator access?* Most cloud providers utilize highly automated deployment methods that require only a minimal caretaker staff in their data centers. However, because of their sheer size, the enormous amounts of compute resources, and their broad customer base, cloud providers probably employ more people with administrator-level access than any single enterprise would. There's no magic tipping point where fewer administrators means better security and more administrators means worse security. And even if there were, this magic number would probably be different for each of the provider's customers. More importantly, what you should get from your provider is an understanding of how they grant, manage, and revoke access and how they log and audit all privilege use.

- *Is the customer permitted to approve any maintenance, updates, or changes?* More than any of its utility-style predecessors, modern cloud computing seeks to maximize the utilization of resources by abstracting and decoupling hardware from applications and data. The kinds of routine maintenance a provider performs—patching host operating systems, for instance—should be done in such a way that the provider's customers will never notice. To receive assurance that you won't experience unplanned downtime, it's perfectly acceptable to ask the provider about their procedures.

Frequently, questionnaires you can download from the Internet were written with a different context in mind (not to mention the risk stance of the questionnaire's author—which probably differs from yours). Cloud computing isn't equivalent to traditional web hosting; questionnaires that are suitable for web hosting providers aren't directly translatable to the cloud. And before you send your questionnaire to your provider, think about each item. Is it relevant? If not, remove it.

IN SUMMARY

Despite the hype, the shift from on-premise computing to the cloud fundamentally alters the way organizations develop and deliver information technology.

It changes the ways you design software, secure information, and manage systems. Processes that once required many months—provisioning servers or testing code changes—can now be completed almost instantaneously. Traditional lifecycle methodologies and control validation processes will similarly evolve and bring about the era of *compliant by inclusion*. Now, an organization can focus its compliance efforts on that which differentiates it from competitors and outsource the remainder to providers. The next few years might very well show increased interest by providers to compete for customers based on who has the better set of validated and attested controls—that would make for interesting times, indeed.

NOTES

1. Props to Bruce Schneier for describing this tradeoff in his essay, "The Psychology of Security," www.schneier.com/essay-155.html.
2. A common best practice is to instrument the scaling mechanism. When the instrumentation reports that your current deployment is reaching maximum scale, your application should slow down new incoming requests while the scaling process adds new resources, because the new resources won't appear instantly. This helps eliminate blackout conditions during the resource provisioning period.
3. http://csrc.nist.gov/publications/nistpubs/800-37-rev1/sp800-37-rev1-final .pdf.
4. www.cloudsecurityalliance.org/cm.html.

CHAPTER FIVE

Cloud-Based IT Service Delivery and Support

Peter Coffee

Perfection is achieved not when there is nothing more to add, but when there is nothing left to take away.

—*Antoine de Saint-Exupéry*

ANY IT OPERATIONS display the same kind of growth rings as an ancient redwood tree, with layer upon layer of accumulated complexity—and with every layer adding new opportunities for security risk or privacy breach, whether due to accidental misconfiguration or deliberate attack.

Every interface is a potential point of error or invasion; adding interfaces to an existing, multilayer model *ipso facto* adds new risks and corresponding costs. It's therefore crucial to recognize that threats to security and privacy are enlarged, not contained, when legacy models are extended past the point where they should have been supplanted—no matter how much effort and expense are applied in pursuit of protection and governance.

 ## BEYOND MERE MIGRATION

A physical migration of a traditional IT model, with attendant addition of new layers and connections, may all too easily become the flawed perception of what the cloud model has to offer. A costly, complex, brittle technology stack that's been moved to a virtualized, supersized environment is still costly to configure and maintain, complex to deploy and upgrade, and brittle in the face of continuing technical and business process change.

Rather than adding yet another layer of costly but fragile perimeter defense or link security, the move to the cloud should instead be viewed as an opportunity to achieve greater strength through radical simplification. The concept of *securely shared* should guide every step of cloud service design and delivery.

When that happens, cloud service customers and their many overseers and stakeholders are often surprised to discover that true clouds reduce many risks, while making others easier to address.

 ## ARCHITECTED TO SHARE, SECURELY

It's not a new idea to centralize IT operations in pursuit of economies of scale. It's not a new idea to locate a centralized facility on the premises of an external service provider, whose presumed concentration of expertise may be hoped to maximize the gains for multiple customer organizations. Well-worn labels like *managed service provider*, or *application service provider*, testify to a decades-long drive to put the undifferentiating grunt work of IT somewhere else—thereby letting a company's own tech talent focus on the creation of competitive advantage, instead of the configuration and maintenance of a commodity IT stack.

There's a fundamental difference, though, between aging notions of outsourcing and the contemporary vision of *cloud computing*. That difference is defined by the actual transformation, rather than mere relocation, of the hardware/software stack. Anyone who proposes to offer a cloud-based service should understand the challenge as well as the opportunity that's involved.

Single-Tenant Offsite Operations (Managed Service Providers)

The simplest way to turn IT from product to service is to have a contractor purchase, configure, install, operate, and maintain hardware and software in a contractor facility, instead of having those IT assets located on enterprise premises and managed by enterprise employees. Such a facility might house many customers' single-tenant stacks, each configured and operated largely independently of the others.

This offers the potential of nearly immediate, but ultimately superficial economies of moving IT installations to a less costly space—perhaps with the sharing of capital-intensive hardware such as backup electrical power, and the hiring of personnel in lower-cost labor markets. Further savings may result from improved utilization of expert skills that may be needed on short notice, but are only infrequently required by any typical organization.

Those savings are offset, though, by any given customer's loss of ability to prioritize operations and maintenance efforts, perhaps resulting in delays to critical system updates or problem resolution processes. When prospects shun the economy of the cloud due to fear of *loss of control*, this is likely to be the specific concern that is on their minds.

Isolated-Tenant Application Services (Application Service Providers)

An enterprise might instead engage multiple service providers, each supporting a single application or perhaps a small multi-application portfolio. Such an application software provider might offer its customers a choice between licensing application code for installation and use on the customer's premises, or subscribing to the use of an application stack that's maintained by the provider at the provider's own site.

An application service provider arrangement offers some gains and some losses, compared to the offsite data center of a managed service provider as described above. An application service provider setup has the potential for efficiencies resulting from a provider maintaining similar instances of similar application stacks, each using many of the same components—although, most likely, with varying capacities. Growing use of virtualization technology may seem to be a logical match for this model: it may be useful to define a single virtualized environment, and to copy and activate as many instances of that virtual appliance as are needed to provide adequate capacity under varying loads.

These potential benefits are offset, though, by difficulties of integrating application function, or sharing data, across both the physical and the architectural boundaries of single-tenant stacks that cannot be expected to share common principles of design—and are likely to be operated at separate locations by uncoordinated teams.

Multitenant (Cloud) Applications and Platforms

Instead of designing a conventional application for either on-premise deployment or isolated-tenancy service delivery, an application provider can begin with a plan to support many separate organizations on a single logical instance of an application or platform—exclusively in a service-provider arrangement. Partitioning of data, rather than being a side effect of deploying multiple instances, must then become the foundation of the application's (or application platform's) design.

Granular Privilege Assignment

It's essential to make this distinction clear. In conventional software design there's an inherent notion of a distinct trust boundary (or a concentric series of such boundaries). In older systems, the logical boundary has typically been implicit in a physical boundary: access to data assets was only enabled from within office walls. More modern systems add technologies such as a *virtual private network* to extend their physical reach; but in either case, privileges outside the boundary are restricted or even completely denied, while privileges inside that boundary are extensive and often unlimited.

As already noted, systems using this legacy model may offer nested levels of privilege, with some users having (for example) read-only access while others enjoy read-write access, and perhaps giving only top-level administrators the privileges of creation and deletion as well; hierarchy, not granularity, is the model in most traditional IT environments, and that simple hierarchy of privilege is well recognized as a source of significant risk. According to results reported in May 2007, by Newton, a Massachusetts-based Cyber-Ark Software, a survey of more than 200 IT professionals found one-third of them actually admitting to abuse of their administrative access privileges to examine sensitive data unrelated to their job functions. About one-fourth reported knowledge of former employees who retained access to "sensitive networks" long after their termination, with one-third stating a belief that they could do likewise with little risk of detection.[1]

Standard Object Permissions

Before assigning this profile to your mobile users, check the online help for the permissions required to access Salesforce remotely using clients such as Force.com Connect Offline.

	Read	Create	Edit	Delete		Read	Create	Edit	Delete
Accounts	✓	✓	✓	✓	Documents	✓	✓	✓	✓
Assets	✓	✓	✓	✓	Leads	✓	✓	✓	✓
Campaigns	✓				Opportunities	✓	✓	✓	✓
Cases	✓	✓	✓		Price Books	✓			
Contacts	✓	✓	✓	✓	Products	✓			
Contracts	✓	✓	✓	✓	Solutions	✓	✓		

Custom Object Permissions

	Read	Create	Edit	Delete		Read	Create	Edit	Delete
Connections	✓	✓	✓	✓	Pledges	✓	✓	✓	✓
Households	✓	✓	✓	✓	Recurring Donations	✓	✓	✓	✓

EXHIBIT 5.1   Privilege Profile Assignment for Customer DataTypes in a Multitenant Database

Compare the risks of such a simple privilege hierarchy to a multitenant design, in which data ownership can (and must) be deep-dyed into individual data elements. In the salesforce.com database, for example, there is no single table in any physical database instance that represents data assets specific to any individual customer organization. Rather, there are millions of data elements, whose individual structure includes a representation of which customer organizations may have access to any given element—further control of which individual subscribers within those organizations can exercise their choice of specific privileges (see Exhibit 5.1).

Any given organization might define several constellations of privilege like the one shown above (such as the *profiles* defined by service administrators at salesforce.com customer organizations): this mechanism enables rapid granting, modification, or revocation of privileges for individual users to correspond with individual roles and responsibilities. By matching comprehensive privilege sets to individuals, rather than issuing application-specific login IDs and passwords that are all too often shared among several users, the multitenant model can improve the effectiveness of many governance measures. Not only the data elements, but also the endpoint locations and even the times of day when access is allowed, can be managed with relative ease.

Consider the further governance improvements that can result from this granularity. There might be tasks, for example, involving data update—such as revising the credit rating of a customer—that do not require the person making the update to know what the previous value of a datum may have been. In a multitenant model of the kind described here, the privilege of editing can be decoupled from the privilege of reading: an employee could have a task-specific user interface that enables entry of new values without visibility of the values being replaced, and without undesirable access to data that the employee's role creates no need to see.

A long-sought goal of IT governance, the granting of privileges as needed by business process rather than as dictated by technology's constraints, is thus brought much closer to achievement.

It's important, though, to anticipate and refute the notion that a multi-tenant system represents *keeping your data in the same database as your competitors.* This chimera is often invoked by vendors of single-tenant offerings, and it's precisely as silly as challenging the systems of a financial, health-care, or telecom service provider that maintains data on each of thousands or millions of account holders or patients. Design, implementation and administration of databases to segregate access to sensitive information is not a bleeding-edge domain, but a mature and trustworthy discipline.

What's new in the cloud computing model is democratization of access to such powerful and efficient resources through subscription service agreements, rather than making these robust and secure systems available only to those who have the capital and human resources to construct and operate a data center of their own.

Inherent Transaction Visibility

Consider further the inherent visibility that's enabled by handling all inter-actions through invocation of service functions, rather than via direct manip-ulation of data items in a representation such as a spreadsheet. When every interaction is a function call to a shared service, it's straightforward to add the option of logging all interactions of any kind that affect any specific type of data (see Exhibit 5.2).

The resulting combination of precise, granular control of access and straightforward logging of data interactions is clearly a boon to efforts such as a response to an HIPAA audit questionnaire. Consider the responses demanded in the first HIPAA audit to be disclosed to the public, performed in March of 2007, and reviewing the state of compliance by Piedmont Hospital in Atlanta, Georgia. In June of that year, *Computerworld* published[2] a list of 42 items to which their source reported a demand that the hospital respond within 10 days: these included a requirement to document policies and

EXHIBIT 5.2 Change History Controls in a Multitenant Database Using Service Invocations

procedures for IT processes, including demands for response on the following representative points as reportedly presented in the demand for response:

- Regularly reviewing records of information system activity, such as audit logs, access reports, and security incident tracking reports.
- Creating, documenting, and reviewing exception reports or logs. Please provide a list of examples of security violation logging and monitoring.
- Establishing security access controls.
- Computer patch management.

Even such a simple phrase as *security access controls* in a questionnaire like the one above, is itself merely the implicit heading of a prospectively lengthy list of technologies and practices such as automatic logout intervals, data encryption, and provisions for emergency access that may require temporary relaxation of everyday access restrictions.

It's therefore far from difficult to envision the overwhelming complexity, cost and uncertainty in a traditional IT environment that would surround a mandate such as, "Recording and examining activity in information systems that contain or use ePHI [electronic Patient Health Information]." In a client-server setting, such information might reside in spreadsheets on individual desktop systems or even on laptop machines that were often taken out of the facility. Such information might be distributed, haphazardly, through email messages and their attachments, with no reliable way of knowing how one person's privilege to retrieve that information might have led to uncontrolled retransmission or unauthorized duplicate storage.

In a cloud environment, the most convenient way to handle such information is also the safest. As famously observed by John Gall in his "Vector Theory of Systems," systems run best when designed to run "downhill"—that is, to make the desired behavior the easiest option available to the user.[3]

A report from a cloud database application can only be viewed by a person who is authorized on the basis of individual access credentials to see it; at the end of the session, the default behavior would be to discard the view of that report as part of the process of shutting down a Web browser, leaving no residual state on the endpoint device (since every popular browser can be configured to flush all local copies of data that have been viewed during a session—a policy readily enforced via system lock-down tools that are already common at many sites).

Further, the fact that a particular user called up a particular report can be centrally logged, jump-starting any subsequent audit in the event that information turns out to have been inappropriately shared or released.

Centralized Community Creation

Next, consider the enormous simplification—and therefore, risk reduction—that results when multiple organizations are customers of a single cloud services provider.

In a traditional legacy IT environment, sharing of data across organization boundaries is tantamount to a process of tunneling out of one fortress, making a journey across open territory, and tunneling into another fortified structure.

All of the apparatus that's been placed around each organization's systems to protect them from accident or malice must be circumvented or nullified (albeit with permission to do so) if those organizations are to share information in any number of useful ways—for example, if a customer of a shipping company is to be given real-time updates on packages in transit, or if a partner company is to share information on an opportunity being jointly pursued.

The proper way to do such things is to write an application that exposes specific data, through specific access methods, subject to specific security protocols and authentications. Sadly, the tempting and common way to do such things is by introducing special-case rules into a company's firewall systems, allowing external access using the equivalent of a secret handshake: a common *security through obscurity* shortcut.

One former FBI data security expert described, to this author, the cumulative result of months or years of such practices by harried developers, trying to meet the urgent demands of business units to enable useful transactions: "It turns your firewall into a fire log," he said, "whose most likely function is to burn you."

A multitenant environment creates an opportunity to do such selective sharing in a manner that is precise, straightforward, and secure. Metadata pockets that are, by default, entirely isolated from each other—specific to individual customer organizations—may be linked on an object-by-object basis, with either read-only or shared read-write privileges being granted by the object's owner to any number of other tenants of the system.

Rather than constructing an elaborate, redundant, and brittle chain of interfaces to overcome another elaborate structure of protections, a metadata-to-metadata link simply adds a specific privilege within the single, coherent trust model that normally enforces separation between the data assets of distinct tenant organizations. Invitations to connect, and mappings of logically equivalent objects that have different names in two different environments, become operations that can be handled by an authorized administrator instead of requiring a more costly technical specialist and a budget for auxiliary software (see Exhibit 5.3).

Links of this kind are quickly created, highly specific in the privileges they confer, and fully protected within the normal process of granting credentials and managing access that's integral to the multitenant model. Rather than being a risky and complex exception, data sharing across organizations becomes a well-behaved extension. This represents a substantial advantage over the difficulties of integrating separate SaaS applications that are being delivered by a legacy-model application service provider in the way described

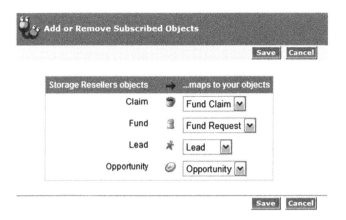

EXHIBIT 5.3   Selective Data Sharing and Object Name Remapping Across Tenant Organizations

near the beginning of this chapter: the older ASP approach preserves and compounds the difficulties of integrating two separate data centers, in addition to preserving the complexities of traditional-model customization, which will now be discussed and contrasted with the cloud approach.

Coherent Customization

If cloud computing merely offered economies of storage, combined with superior access control to valuable data, these would not be trivial benefits—but they merely set the table, so to speak, for a multicourse meal of powerful applications that enjoy similar transformational advantages.

The metadata pools that contain and segregate data, customer by customer, can also contain metadata representations of customized application function: workflows, application-specific business logic, data validation rules, and any number of other useful extensions to an otherwise generic application platform.

There are fundamental reasons why metadata-driven design is essential for breakthrough economies and accelerations of business process development. In the traditional IT environment, customization of an off-the-shelf application takes place in the same logical space—that is, the realm of application code—that houses the code base provided by the application vendor. It's commonly recognized, and even considered by many to be unavoidable, that customization therefore contaminates vendor code, turning something that began as an off-the-shelf product into a customer-specific derivative of that product.

The consequence of this code-level customization is a sword that cuts both ways. The customer incurs substantial cost and risk from any major vendor upgrade that might disrupt the function of laboriously crafted customizations: extensive testing is necessary, and considerable rework may be required before an upgrade can be deployed. Customers, therefore, postpone their acceptance and deployment of vendor upgrades, a cruel irony given that customers' maintenance fees to the vendor are a major source of funding for upgrades' development.

At the same time, vendors confront a marketplace in which only a fraction of their current customers are actually using the current product. Costs such as development and issuance of security updates for N *minus 1* or N *minus 2* (or even older) product versions, and continuing user support for long-deprecated features, continue to burden the vendor and dilute the resources available for product improvement—further diminishing value to the customer. It will be noted, for example, that Microsoft's Windows XP continued to run a majority of the world's desktop computers more than nine years after its initial release, despite the subsequent release of both the Windows Vista and Windows 7 operating systems, each of which represented enormous investments of software development effort.

Finally, in the specific context of issues of security and privacy, code-level customization implies low-level access to application behavior: in this typical environment, every individual developer in an enterprise application development shop is potentially the weak link that compromises the security posture of an entire application portfolio. No piece of the portfolio is too innocuous to be a potential concern: in one global challenge, for example, the successful attacker (in a competition conducted by the journal *eWEEK*) was able to penetrate a core database through a pathway created by a privilege escalation shortcut in an online help system.

When cloud services use and adhere to a metadata-based design, there is an absolute distinction between the code space controlled by the service provider and the metadata space controlled by customer organizations. A customer application at the metadata level simply cannot compromise the security of the code layer, any more than a misspelled word in a document can compromise the password protection mechanism of a word processor.

Meanwhile, multitenant application portfolios and platforms can introduce significant upgrades while bringing forward the customers' specializations without disruption. Development effort, including continual improvement of security mechanisms and practices, is entirely focused on a single code base, rather than being spread across the archeological strata of past releases.

THE QUESTION OF LOCATION

It's common, in any cloud computing conversation, to encounter the question of "where will my data reside?" In some cases, this is driven by concern regarding regulation or legislation. In some cases, it's driven by a desire to assure the secondary customers of the service customer that personal data is not traveling to parts unknown.

A cloud service provider should be able to tell a customer that data can reside wherever the customer prefers. There are reasons why any of several options might be chosen:

- If a customer stores data in the service provider's multitenant environment, it can be protected by the provider's (presumably) rigorous tools and practices, subject to the costly certifications that a provider will find it necessary to obtain as a cost of being competitive. These might include ISO 27001, SAS70 Type II, SSAE 16 Type II, SysTrust, and other such seals of approval.

- A multitenant system may also be designed to give customers additional flexibility in choosing, field by field, whether data will be further encrypted. One must expect that an encrypted field will be unavailable for use as a key in generating reports, and that it will not be subject to searching or sorting operations, but many types of data have no need of such facilities—e.g., credit card numbers—and may therefore be candidates for this added protection.

- Alternatively, cloud services can provide integration facilities that allow a customer to locate data external to the cloud provider's systems. A customer might continue, for example, to use on-premise ERP as the primary system of record, while using a cloud application platform and/or multiparty compositions of cloud services to develop and deploy new applications that liberate additional business value from that data.

   In this situation, a customer might create a token such as an Account ID number that has no legal or regulatory significance, and use that token to identify a collection of other attributes such as order frequency and size; a cloud application could then apply algorithms of choice to identify key accounts by any desired means, then return the list of token values to be reassociated (within the customer organization's firewall) with sensitive information such as bank references or tax IDs.

Initially, it is likely that customers will be more interested in the benefits of the cloud when they understand that they retain considerable freedom to locate data where they choose. Over time, customers tend to become more comfortable with application development options that seem too risky when they're new to the market: every argument that's made today against the public cloud was being made, 15 years ago, about the use of the public Internet instead of proprietary EDI networks to handle transactional and other critical workloads.

In time, compelling economics shift people into the mode of looking for ways to make something work—instead of seeking, understandably, excuses to delay a disruptive change.

DESIGNED AND DELIVERED FOR TRUST

Earlier in this chapter, it was acknowledged that many prospective customers of cloud services are put off by the perception of losing control. Regardless of objective technical or economic benefits, there may be a deeply felt belief that unforeseen circumstances—"unknown unknowns," in the words of Donald Rumsfeld[4]—must always be envisioned, and that these situations will expose a cloud service adopter to criticism (or worse) if it's perceived that critical functions were unwisely trusted to others.

Cloud service providers *must* acknowledge and address, not dismiss, these concerns, because services are sold to people, and service providers must therefore be as much psychologists as they are technologists.

Fewer Points of Failure

It should first be observed, and communicated effectively to service customers, that the cloud model dramatically reduces the number of potential points of failure compared to traditional on-premise or outsourced IT deployment and delivery. In single-tenant systems, regardless of where they are located, every component of every instance of a software stack is a potential source of trouble; cloud systems have far fewer distinct stacks with far fewer components.

On-premise electronic mail systems, for example, typically come with a vendor recommendation to put fewer than 1,000 mailbox accounts on each processor core: in a 10,000-person organization, this may require on the order of three quad-core processors, each representing its own configuration of an operating system and an application stack that must be updated and patched in a continuing series of maintenance operations. Moreover, this is just for the single function of providing electronic mail.

Virtualization may reduce some aspects of this problem: a single "virtual appliance" template can be instantiated as many times as needed to handle peak workloads, then flushed from the system to re-allocate that capacity. This reduces the number of independent opportunities for error. One must be aware, though, of the potential for a virtualization template to calcify an insecure configuration, and to re-introduce (whenever that template is reactivated) a vulnerability that was thought to have been *patched out* of an IT portfolio. Patch management tools and procedures may fail to identify and maintain virtual machines or dormant *virtual machine* definitions.[5]

Cloud services using multitenant models shrink these problems on two dimensions:

1. First, the number of separate instances is hugely reduced: salesforce.com, for example, as of March 2011, was running a variety of workloads for nearly 100,000 organizations on only 23 instances of the company's core service engine, deployed in hardware *pods* comprising (in aggregate) only a few thousand standard x86 servers.

   Microsoft executive Craig Mundie has estimated that it would require at least 100,000 servers to deliver the same capability using a traditional on-premise approach.[6] The efficiencies of multitenant cloud delivery thus shrink the burden of server management by (conservatively) one or two orders of magnitude.

2. Second, the coherence of the code base is greatly improved. As discussed above, the traditional approach leads to proliferation of multiple versions of a single software product within an IT portfolio. At Bechtel Corporation, for example, CIO Geir Ramleth's internal inventory found as many as five distinct versions of an application in use by different business units.[7] A multitenant cloud service will, in general, be running only a single code base, preserving customers' freedom to modify behavior—or even to postpone indefinitely the acceptance of an upgrade feature—by mechanisms operating at the metadata layer, as described above.

   This is a crucial point of understanding, as to the difference between consumer Web applications (typically having limited ability to customize) and enterprise cloud services. Any notion that cloud services impose their upgrades on a vendor-driven schedule should be rebutted, explicitly, by

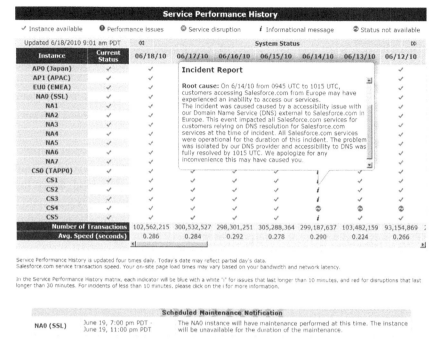

Service Performance History								
✓ Instance available	❶ Performance issues	☺ Service disruption	*i* Informational message			☺ Status not available		

Updated 6/18/2010 9:01 am PDT	«			System Status				»
Instance	**Current Status**	06/18/10	06/17/10	06/16/10	06/15/10	06/14/10	06/13/10	06/12/10
AP0 (Japan)	✓	✓						✓
AP1 (APAC)	✓	✓						✓
EU0 (EMEA)	✓	✓						✓
NA0 (SSL)	✓	✓						✓
NA1	✓	✓						✓
NA2	✓	✓						✓
NA3	✓	✓						✓
NA4	✓	✓						✓
NA5	✓	✓						✓
NA6	✓	✓						✓
NA7	✓	✓						✓
CS0 (TAPP0)	✓	✓	✓	✓	✓	*i*	✓	✓
CS1	✓	✓	✓	✓	✓	*i*	✓	✓
CS2	✓	✓	✓	✓	✓	*i*	✓	✓
CS3	✓	✓	✓	✓	✓	*i*	✓	✓
CS4	✓	✓	✓	✓	✓	☺	☺	☺
CS5	✓	✓	✓	✓	✓	*i*	✓	✓
Number of Transactions		102,562,215	300,532,527	298,301,251	305,288,364	299,187,637	103,482,159	93,154,869
Avg. Speed (seconds)		0.286	0.284	0.292	0.278	0.290	0.224	0.266

> **Incident Report**
>
> **Root cause:** On 6/14/10 from 0945 UTC to 1015 UTC, customers accessing Salesforce.com from Europe may have experienced an inability to access our services. The incident was caused caused by a accessibility issue with our Domain Name Service (DNS) external to Salesforce.com in Europe. This event impacted all Salesforce.com services for customers relying on DNS resolution for Salesforce.com services at the time of incident. All Salesforce.com services were operational for the duration of this incident. The problem was isolated by our DNS provider and accessibility to DNS was fully resolved by 1015 UTC. We apologize for any inconvenience this may have caused you.

Service Performance History is updated four times daily. Today's date may reflect partial day's data.
Salesforce.com service transaction speed. Your on-site page load times may vary based on your bandwidth and network latency.

In the Service Performance History matrix, each indicator will be blue with a white "i" for issues that last longer than 10 minutes, and red for disruptions that last longer than 30 minutes. For incidents of less than 10 minutes, please click on the i for more information.

Scheduled Maintenance Notification		
NA0 (SSL)	June 19, 7:00 pm PDT - June 19, 11:00 pm PDT	The NA0 instance will have maintenance performed at this time. The instance will be unavailable for the duration of the maintenance.

EXHIBIT 5.4 Public Disclosure of Service Operational Status and Anomalies Improves Customer Trust

communicating options for customers to preview and (if desired) defer upgrade acceptance using metadata configuration tools.

Visibility and Transparency

Also of note is the high standard of near-real-time reporting of cloud service anomalies, exhibited by cloud services such as salesforce.com, Amazon Web Services, and Google. All three of these pure-cloud providers maintain public web sites that report any departure from normal operation, as well as providing best available projections of problem resolution (see Exhibit 5.4).

IN SUMMARY

All too often, discussions of security and privacy focus on denial of unauthorized access. If this were the only relevant measure of success, IT systems would not be connected to external networks at all—any more than companies would take payments by check, let alone accept credit cards, if pure risk reduction were their only concern. Every business decision is a matter of risk identification, assessment, and mitigation in pursuit of prudent profit maximization.

The cloud creates no risks that are fundamentally new; rather, it materially assists in key risk management goals, including providing customer assurance and satisfying applicable laws and regulations.

Marketplace pressures are driving the enterprise toward greater connectivity and richer interaction with external systems, ranging from supply-chain integrations to customer-facing facilities for taking orders and delivering customer support. Adding this connectivity and interaction to traditional IT models destroys the *de facto* security perimeters created by physical isolation of IT systems, and forces the enterprise to re-envision its approach to data and process protection.

Cloud models can radically streamline many of the legacy complexities, and corresponding vulnerabilities that have accumulated during decades of incremental progress in IT capability. Fewer points of failure, greater visibility of operation, granular control of privileges, and superior auditability of actions performed are among the benefits that can be offered by cloud service providers—as long as they fully adopt the cloud, rather than merely repackaging a legacy IT model in *cloudish* form.

 ## NOTES

1. CAS, Survey Reveals Scandal of Snooping IT Staff (press release issued May 30, 2007, by Cyber-Ark Software, Ltd.), www.cyber-ark.com/news-events/pr_20070530.asp (acccessed March 18, 2011).

2. J. Vijayan, HIPAA Audit: The 42 Questions HHS Might Ask (2007), www.computerworld.com/s/article/9025253/HIPAA_audit_The_42_questions_HHS_might_ask (accessed March 18, 2011).

3. J. Gall, Applied Systemantics I: Practical Systems Design (1975), www2.ece.ohio-state.edu/~fasiha/systemantics/#CH10 (accessed March 18, 2011).

4. D. Rumsfeld, DoD News Briefing—Secretary Rumsfeld and Gen. Myers (2002), www.defense.gov/transcripts/transcript.aspx?transcriptid=2636 (accessed March 18, 2011).

5. J. Brodkin, Virtual Server Sprawl Highlights Security Concerns (2008), www.networkworld.com/news/2008/043008-interop-virtual-server-sprawl.html (accessed March 18, 2011).

6. V. Barret, The Next Battle Against Microsoft: Salesforce.com CEO Marc Benioff on the New Frontier in Business Software (2010), www.forbes.com/2010/05/05/benioff-microsoft-facebook-intelligent-technology-salesforce.html (accessed March 18, 2011).
7. S. Overby, Bechtel's New Benchmarks (2008), www.cio.com/article/456588/Bechtel_s_New_Benchmarks (accessed March 18, 2011).

CHAPTER SIX

Protection and Privacy of Information Assets in the Cloud

Nikhil Kumar
Leon DuPree

No one shall be subjected to arbitrary interference with his privacy, family, home, or correspondence, nor to attacks upon his honor and reputation. Everyone has the right to the protection of the law against such interference or attacks.

—Article 12 of the Declaration of Human Rights, UN, 1948

ONE OF THE most significant barriers to entry for the adoption of cloud computing is the impact of security and the protection and privacy of information assets in the cloud.[1] Thus, for the security, IT, or business professionals pursuing the adoption of cloud solutions, it is important to understand what differentiates cloud solutions, what is relevant from a data protection and privacy context, what are the potential legal and compliance implications, and how to approach the deployment or creation of cloud solutions.

In fact, there are three scenarios to be considered within the context of the cloud: how an organization *consuming* cloud-based solutions deals with the privacy and protection of information assets and incorporates this into its due diligence and cost and risk assessment as it adopts cloud-based solutions, how an organization *providing* cloud solutions deals with the privacy and protection of information assets, including their monitoring and risk management, especially keeping in mind the rapid and ongoing evolution of laws, and how *regulatory* organizations audit cloud solutions.

To be able to understand the protection and privacy of information assets in the cloud, it is important to understand what constitutes a cloud environment. To establish this context, we refer to prior work from NIST[2] and Nikhil Kumar[3] and define key *cloud characteristics* that are features of a cloud implementation.

These cloud characteristics enable us to distinguish a cloud context from other traditional IT contexts and define what constitutes and differentiates cloud solutions (offerings) (and by association, data in the cloud) from traditional solutions. These characteristics are then further refined by criteria associated with movement of the cloud from one cloud deployment model to another (e.g., private cloud to public cloud).

This forms the basis for our definition of a *cloud security reference model*, which addresses both *data at rest* and *data in flight*.

Due to the binary nature of cloud assets in general, we consider information assets to be *software* information assets, and privacy to refer to *information (data)* privacy in the context of data stored in binary form. As such, we use the term *data* interchangeably with *information* throughout this chapter. We do not consider traditional record keeping and other forms of information in the context of cloud consumers and providers to be within scope, though it is possible that cloud providers may maintain data in that form driven by implementation models and business requirements.

Having established the context, we then review legal aspects, state of industry standards, and regulatory specifications. From there, we look at how the aforementioned apply and establish a baseline for data privacy and security legislation. This covers data security and privacy standards, data classification schemes and governance standards, and their implications in the context of the three scenarios. Cloud computing is a very disruptive technology, having profound social and legal connotations. It represents the true migration to the digital age, where data becomes commoditized and the context of personal space extends into the virtual world: Where do my privacy rights end—in my house or in my *virtual* house? This question is being asked and answered through acts of jurisprudence and is in a tremendous flux. Our chapter would not be complete without reviewing this, as it is a necessary part of the context. Traditional views of notice and choice are being challenged,[4] and because of the global nature of the cloud it is important to think about the topic in a global context.

We then try to answer the question, how do I *use* this information? The question of data privacy and security needs to be answered from the context of the three perspectives: *cloud consumer, cloud provider,* and *regulator.* To help use the privacy and information protection information from a practitioner perspective we provide a cloud *data privacy and security playbook* to help cloud stakeholders use this information. The playbook will need to be tailored by users to meet regulatory and industrial guidelines based on the line of business and solution being followed.

Finally, we describe the future direction and the evolution of data and privacy in the cloud.

 ## THE THREE USAGE SCENARIOS

The three usage scenarios to be considered within the context of the cloud are for organizations *consuming* cloud-based solutions, *providing* cloud solutions, and *regulating* cloud solutions. In this document, we are only focused on the concept of regulator from a protection of assets and privacy perspective.

Thus there are three points of view that we need to consider as we review the asset protection and privacy in a cloud context—those of the consumer, the provider, and the regulator.

From the consumer's point of view, the following questions need to be considered:

- How do I do my due diligence when deploying to the cloud?
- What are the associated costs?
- What risk is posed to the organization if the cloud vendor were to vanish (vendor lock-in)?
- What risk is there from an ongoing monitoring and audit perspective when the cloud solution is in use?
- When I am done, how do I de-provision and transition assets out of the cloud vendor to another location or context?

From the cloud provider's point of view the following questions need to be considered:

- What will be the cost to me to provision and de-provision assets?
- What happens when data privacy laws change?
- How do I manage the security of assets?
- What are my risks (both ethical and legal) if, in my role as cloud provider, I am in possession of information assets, and other organizations such as the government ask for, directly or indirectly, access to information assets? What data protection and monitoring needs are there?
- What commitments do I need to make in the context of data integrity?
- How do I provide access to regulators without any risk to privacy or loss of protection of the assets in my care?
- What are my responsibilities toward these assets?

It is important to note that these issues are already significantly impacting cloud providers, with a myriad of data breaches[5] impacting the cloud, as seen in the case of the Google cloud data security issue[6] and the farmer bankruptcy case.[7]

From the regulator's point of view, there needs to be the ability to review and access audit data to manage and ensure that controls are in place and have been used for information assets, keeping in mind data privacy and protections laws that are rapidly evolving. Furthermore, as our virtual world grows in importance and scope, the protection of information assets and their privacy within national and international laws now involve law and order, national security, defense, and intelligence—issues which often conflict with freedom and privacy.

WHAT IS A CLOUD? ESTABLISHING THE CONTEXT—DEFINING CLOUD SOLUTIONS AND THEIR CHARACTERISTICS

So what is a cloud? To quote the NIST,[8] "Cloud computing is a model for enabling convenient, on-demand network access to a shared pool of configurable computing resources (e.g., networks, servers, storage, applications, and services) that can be rapidly provisioned and released with minimal management effort or service provider interaction." We believe that cloud computing is a particular architectural style, which is a derivative of the SOA style. The SOA architecture style is defined by the Open Group[9] as having a set of clearly defined attributes covering the business nature, the use of open standards and interoperability, the need to express the SOA implementation in the context of the specific requirement, strong governance and the need for a litmus test, which requires a good service. The cloud model extends SOA by strengthening some requirements, such as governance becoming important and adding cloud characteristics such as elasticity and locality independence. In particular, a fundamental premise of the cloud is that cloud solutions deal with *managed services*.

Cloud solutions can be thought of as falling into three or more service models,[10] which differ in terms of *levels of abstraction*. The commonly accepted ones are Infrastructure as a Service (IaaS), Platform as a Service (PaaS), and Software as a Service (SaaS). We add Business Process as a Service (BPaaS) model to the list, to reflect scenarios where organizations can define business process abstractions and compose them to constitute solutions for the enterprise. Cloud solutions can be further categorized by deployment models,[11] into private, public, hybrid, and community clouds. Along with these two dimensions (those of deployment and service models), there are *cloud characteristics* (such as *elasticity* and *locality independence*), which typify cloud solutions.

Assessing the characteristics in the context of the models helps stakeholders determine the best fit, the risk, and the implications from a protection and privacy perspective. Exhibit 6.1 outlines this view.

Based on the belief that cloud solutions are a derivative of the SOA architectural style with distinguishing characteristics that are uniquely *cloud* in nature, a cloud reference architecture shares many of the key architectural components described in a SOA. It can thus be treated as an extension of an SOA reference architecture.

What Makes a Cloud Solution?

What makes a solution a *cloud* solution? How do we define what distinguishes a cloud solution from other solutions and architectural styles? Cloud solutions are characterized by a set of *unique characteristics*. NIST has defined five of them,[12] and Gartner another five.[13] We extend these further, and define the cloud characteristics in the context of the perspectives of the consumer, provider, and regulator. The characteristics also reflect *capabilities* that cloud stakeholders need to support.

We believe that the characteristics need to be agnostic of the *implementation* (which is why we do not include *resource pooling* and *uses of Internet*

EXHIBIT 6.1 Characteristics of a Cloud

Cloud Characteristics	NIST	Gartner	Consumer Perspective	Provider Perspective	Regulator Perspective
		Service Based	Service Based	Service Based	Auditability
	On-Demand Self-Service		On-Demand Self-Service	On-Demand Self-Service	Auditability
	Broad Network Access		Broad Network Access	Broad Network Access	
	Rapid Elasticity	Scalable and Elastic	Scalable and Elastic	Scalable and Elastic	
				Unpredictable Demand Demand Servicing Resource Pooling	
	Resource Pooling	Shared	Managed Shared Service	Managed Shared Service	
			Auditability	Auditability	Auditability
			Service Termination and Rollback	Service Termination and Rollback	Auditability of Compliance and Data Deprovisioning
		Metered by Use	Charge by QoS and Use	Metered for Quality of Service	
				Monitor and Account for Use	Accounting and Control

Measured Service	Uses Internet Technologies	Location Independence	Location Independence	Location Independence
		Compensation for Location Independence	Compensation for Location Independence	Auditability
		Multitenancy	Multitenancy	Auditability of Co-Mingling
		Security Characteristics:	Security Characteristics:	
		Confidentiality	Confidentiality	
		Integrity	Integrity	
		Authenticity	Authenticity	
		Accounting and Control	Accounting and Control	
		Collaboration Oriented Architecture	Collaboration Oriented Architecture	
		Federated Access and Identity Management	Federated Access and Identity Management	

103

technologies) and focus on the capabilities that they support. Exhibit 6.1 lists them, grouping associated capabilities together. Since the consumer is the entity being serviced, in general, the grid should be read from left to right (Consumer/Provider/Regulator), though it is possible for there to be characteristics for the provider and regulator that are not dependent on the consumer (e.g., Broad Network Access).

Understanding the Characteristics

For each characteristic, we describe its implications for each of the three perspectives and information protection and privacy.

Service Based

All cloud offerings can be expressed as a service. A service has a contract, which defines its functional and syntactic behavior, as well as commits to quality of service, usage, and elasticity. For both consumers and providers, the implication is the ability to integrate with mechanisms for services to be monitored, metered, and used. This makes the driving criteria interoperability and consistency of the service offering (implying a limitation of customization for consumers). For regulators, the implications are the need for the ability to review and validate the policies (constraints) for the service, and audit of the usage in terms of protection and privacy. Associated characteristics are *on-demand self-service*, and *broad network access*.

On-Demand Self-Service

From a provider perspective it is the ability to support continuous availability (being on all the time), protocols and patterns for self-service. Providers also need to be able to support monitoring and audit of usage. Regulators need to be able to access and review those logs (making interoperability an important architectural constraint).

Broad Network Access

Cloud providers must expect their solutions to provide broad network access, so that their consumers can access them. For providers and consumers, the privacy and protection implication is the need to support security controls for access, confidentiality, and integrity, in a verifiable manner and in an interoperable format.

Scalable and Elastic

All cloud offerings must support the ability to scale, and to meet potentially unpredictable customer demands. They should support elasticity, with the ability to provide the resources without changes in the consumer Quality of Service Service Level Agreements (QoS SLA), in a seamless and on-demand fashion. In particular, *elasticity is the ability to grow and contract as needed.* Cloud providers need to create solutions that meet the consumers' quality of service expectations in a real-time manner with the potential for large increases in volumes and including potentially unforeseeable events. There are no specific privacy and protection implications, except that added resources to provide elasticity meet the required protection and privacy criteria. Associated characteristics are *unpredictable demand*, *demand servicing*, and *resource pooling.*

Unpredictable Demand

Demand in a cloud context is potentially unpredictable in volume.

Demand Servicing

The ability to identify and enable service capabilities required to service unpredictable demand, while meeting QoS commitments in a seamless manner to the consumer.

Resource Pooling

Cloud providers need to be able to support elasticity and scalability in an efficacious and high-performing manner, using resource pooling as one of the architectural principles.

Managed Shared Service

All cloud offerings essentially are composed of managed shared services and as such share their attributes for support of usage metering, monitoring, and quality of service. From a privacy and protection perspective, consumers need to be able to define the related policies, which in turn need to be defined in an interoperable standards compliant manner that providers can service. Regulators need access to this data.

Auditability

Auditability is the ability of cloud solutions to provide an audit of information use through its lifecycle in a *verifiable*, *usable*, and *accessible* manner. It is a prerequisite for the effective use of cloud resources, to know who has accessed information assets and how they have been accessed. It protects the consumer from risk as well as from a charge model perspective—what did I use? who used it? etc. Providers, too, need to provide for auditability, while regulators need to use the auditability of solutions to be able to effectively conduct audits. Key attributes are the interoperability of formats of audit records, and the protection of *personally identifiable information* (PII) and sensitive information using approaches such as obfuscation and de-identification, guaranteeing that auditing is done and records are available across all stages of the information lifecycle, and that the structure is in place for auditability to work (e.g., *data classification* and *information lifecycle policies*, etc.).

Service Termination and Rollback

The ability to seamlessly terminate and rollback a service is important for cloud usage, for both consumers and providers. Consumers want the ability to deal with vendor changes, while providers need to be able to deal with the risk of stale data being left with them and the associated risk. Regulators need to be able to ensure that service termination and rollback addresses privacy and protection constraints.

This implies that contracts must support termination and rollback, that there should be interoperability and mechanisms in place to carry this out, and that there should be the ability to ensure that data is de-provisioned in a verifiable manner.

Charge by Quality of Service and Use

The ability to pay for a service on-demand, based on contract characteristics of quality of service, and quantity of use, are characteristics of the cloud. This requires consumers to have the ability to support real-time or near-real-time auditing and accounting of the service in an interoperable manner. Providers need to provide solutions that either expose the solution to mechanisms for metering for QoS and use, or provide the capability themselves. Associated characteristics are the *capability to monitor and quantify use* and *monitor and enforce service policies*.

Capability to Monitor and Quantify Use

Cloud providers need to be able to monitor all aspects of the service, at all stages of its lifetime and quantify its use.

Monitor and Enforce Service Policies

Cloud providers need to be able to monitor and enforce service policies, and provide the capability to enforce policies.

Location Independence: Location Independence implies that cloud services and information are independent of location. Location independence is one of the fundamental characteristics of cloud solutions. From a privacy and protection perspective, this is in conflict with many existing laws. The implication for this is that consumers and provides alike must provide verifiable and auditable commitments to meet location independence in a manner that meets compliance requirements. Providers need to be able to support monitoring of the residency of information and ensuring that appropriate controls are in place as information moves across geographical boundaries, while consumers, and eventually regulators, need to be able to audit and verify compliance. Thus, the associated characteristic is *compensation for location independence*.

Compensation for Location Independence

Cloud providers need to support the ability to maintain location independence in a seamless fashion while keeping data privacy concerns in perspective. For example, a provider providing storage IaaS with infrastructure in the United States and Canada will need to ensure that data migrating across the infrastructure *can legally do so* and is adequately protected. Consumers, on the other hand, need to be able to receive audit information, conduct audits, and in general, be able to meet governance and compliance requirements for where the data is as well as assess whether it meets the requisite privacy and protection policies at any point in its lifecycle. Regulators need to be able to not only receive this information; they also need to be able to process it. This is important, because the volume of data received is going to be huge, so having adequate mechanisms and tooling to be able to do this is going to be a significant aspect of regulators and consumers having the ability to do what is necessary.

Multitenancy

Multitenancy is the ability to have multiple consumers leverage shared resources. While controls and technology exist to separate access, concerns to the co-mingling of PII data are significant. This risk of co-mingling and the shared nature of the resource (even though there are many levels of multitenancy)[14] make it very difficult, if not impossible to address privacy and protection concerns in a verifiable manner when there is multitenancy.

Authentication and Authorization

Varying cloud models have varying authentication and authorization abilities. Trust establishment with multiple domains and circles of trust, and federated authentication is a required feature of cloud solutions. Providers and consumers need to be able to interoperate keeping in mind the specific constraints required by the data. Regulators need to be able to know the *who, how,* and *what* of information access.

Confidentiality

The confidentiality of information assets, including the warranty that no unauthorized individuals and systems access them is a critical feature of cloud solutions. One of the issues is that there is insufficient precedent and legislation in place to effectively define confidentiality in the context of the cloud. For providers, who are accountable for or responsible for data in flight and at rest and managing interactions with downstream service providers, the need to provide *non-repudiable confidentiality* is essential. Reputation, which is critical for providers, is dependent on the appropriate confidentiality criteria being met.

Integrity

Due to the typical scenario where cloud providers become proxy data owners, integrity definition and implementation is a part of the responsibility of the cloud service provider and a part of the quality of service attributes of the managed services provided by the cloud provider. Since, in most cases, the consumer is in the end accountable for the information asset, the reputational impact of integrity impacts both the consumer as well as the provider.

Authenticity

It is important for cloud providers to be able to support non-repudiable authenticity (i.e., it should be able to ensure that all actors who access the data can be audited and the appropriate authorization constraints are in place, and that all transactions support non-repudiation).

Availability

Cloud solutions, in particular, need to meet QoS commitments for shared services. This needs to be adequately accounted for and monitored. There are no significant privacy and protection implications.

Accounting and Control

The need for the metering of cloud services for their use (irrespective of the specific business model) is a key driver for accounting. We believe that in the context of the cloud, audit and accounting are closely related—we need the ability to capture data for audit to ensure that accounting is appropriately implemented. Based on the type of service provided and the service model, this may need to be done in real-time. Service contracts need to specify accounting criteria and controls, which should include privacy and protection policies.

Collaboration Oriented Architecture

The need to be able to deal with relationships (obligations), reputation and business events, and to interact with other systems to form a service chain, as well as manage service interaction are the major characteristics of a cloud solution. In practice, we believe that a Collaboration Oriented Architecture (COA) is essential for the practical, successful implementation of the cloud. Security principles associated with it are defined in the Jericho Forums paper on Collaboration Oriented Architecture.[15] The privacy and protection implications are significant—consumers need to establish constraints for privacy and protections, providers need to be able to meet them, and regulators need to be able to verify that they are followed. For example, if medical records maintained by a cloud-based provider are compromised, the reputational business implications to both the consumer and service provider are significant.

Federated Access and ID Management

The ability to share and manage identity and credentials in a seamless and secure manner is very important for being able to secure information assets in a cloud context. Having separate stores for information assets and managing them in a distributed fashion leads to many potential points of failure and also leaves a human factor open: How often will you forget and potentially send secure information over insecure protocols, or store them in insecure places? How many providers have the competency and capabilities to manage secured federated identities and credentials? We believe that cloud solutions will have cloud services for secure federated identity management over time, potentially from third-party providers. This capability will also need to support user provisioning and de-provisioning.

THE CLOUD SECURITY CONTINUUM AND A CLOUD SECURITY REFERENCE MODEL

Now that we have defined the cloud and its important characteristics, we define the *security reference model*. A security reference model for the cloud must take into context where the data comes from and how it was transported, that is, the context of data in flight and data at rest. Nikhil Kumar[16] presented a reference model that illustrates this model in the context of SOA, which has been extended in the context of the cloud. As can be seen in the Exhibit 6.2, the cloud is composed of cloud consumers who are serviced by services that might, in turn, invoke other services to provide the eventual capability requested by the consumer.

The *Cloud Security Continuum* (the Continuum) model covers the entire set of interactions between a cloud consumer and provider, and gives us a formal basis to understand and review the relationships between participants in the model in the context of security.

The **Security Continuum** extends across the *Consumer* and *Provider* aspects of the cloud. This includes Data in *Flight* and *Rest*.

Security is *a cross-cutting* concern that applies across the *Security Continuum*

Data Privacy also cross-cuts and applies across the continuum

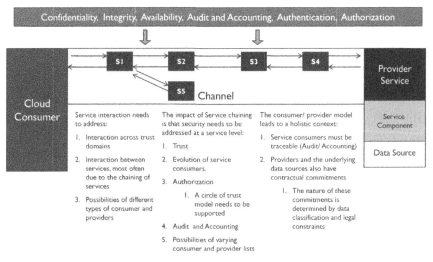

EXHIBIT 6.2 Security in the Context of the Cloud: The Cloud Security Continuum

The Continuum is composed of *security service flows* (also referred to as *service chains* or *flows*), which are composed of *atomic security continuum elements* (referred to as *elements*). Each element is composed of a *consumer* and *provider*. Each consumer has an *end point*, which provides the point of integration with the information that is sent across the channel from a provider end point, into the security trust domain of the consumer. We consider privacy and protection constraints within the context of a consumer's domain to be analogous to traditional constraints for any system, and out of the scope of this chapter.

This model modularizes the Continuum, allowing us to define a privacy and protection definition process, which is further elaborated in the playbook later in the chapter. It is based on the atomicity of a continuum element, which requires a consumer to only know its immediate provider (analogous to the law of Demeter.)[17] This loosely couples the elements in the flows, separating policy definition and enforcement, so that the initiating consumer does not need to know how each provider down the security service flow has implemented privacy and protection, but only its immediate provider. Privacy and protection constraints can then be defined by the initiating provider, but their enforcement delegated to the next consumer in the security elements further down the chain. Juan[18] has shown the value of such an approach in the case of the mitigation of risk toward information protection and privacy (see Exhibit 6.3). We call this the *principle of atomicity*. In practice, this may be the only option available to consumers.

The model for an individual security continuum atomic element supports the separating out of infrastructure to implement the constraints, and allows standards and best practice security design principles, such as those in the Jericho Forum's 12 Commandments[19] to be applied. (See Exhibit 6.4.)

To round off our reference model, we model the security continuum element. Each element is further composed of some basic components, which address the protection and privacy constraints of the cloud. Exhibit 6.5 illustrates this model. As can be seen in this exhibit, an element can be considered to be a combination of the following: *providers* who provide cloud services; *consumers* who consume these services; *policy enforcement points* (PEPs), which validate and enforce that the quality of service is met; *monitors* (*policy monitoring point* or PMP), which meter the usage; and *resources*, which are accessed and used by the *service*. *Quality of service attributes* form the set of *privacy and protection policies* used in the element.

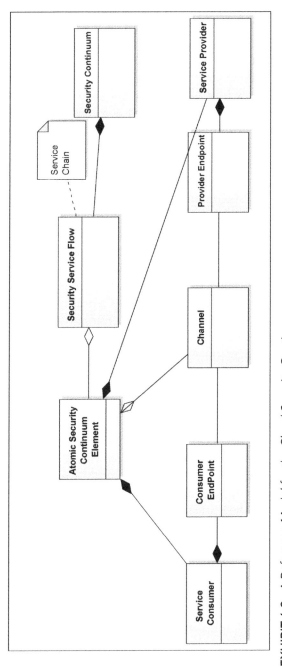

EXHIBIT 6.3 A Reference Model for the Cloud Security Continuum

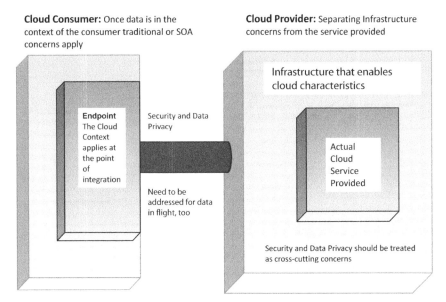

Cloud Consumer: Once data is in the context of the consumer traditional or SOA concerns apply

Cloud Provider: Separating Infrastructure concerns from the service provided

Infrastructure that enables cloud characteristics

Endpoint The Cloud Context applies at the point of integration

Security and Data Privacy

Need to be addressed for data in flight, too

Actual Cloud Service Provided

Security and Data Privacy should be treated as cross-cutting concerns

EXHIBIT 6.4 Cloud Security—An Element at a Time

CLOUD CHARACTERISTICS, DATA CLASSIFICATION, AND INFORMATION LIFECYCLE MANAGEMENT

Now that we have an understanding of cloud characteristics and a security reference model (the Cloud Security Continuum), we review how cloud characteristics map to protection and the privacy of information assets. We also look at the implications of the cloud in the context of information lifecycle management (ILM) as well as the role of data classification in the context of the cloud.

Cloud Characteristics and Privacy and the Protection of Information Assets

The impact of cloud characteristics varies across combinations of cloud service and deployment models, with cloud characteristics acting as constraints for decision points, to pick one combination over the other for a particular cloud solution (offering). The matrix below shows the different types of cloud abstraction and the types of clouds and lists the characteristics most relevant for each cell in the context of privacy and protection.

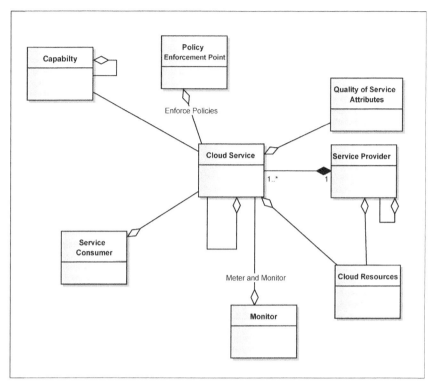

EXHIBIT 6.5 The Reference Model for an Atomic Security Continuum Element

Note the following for Exhibit 6.6:

1. *Information Protection and Privacy* is referred to as IP & P.
2. In general, all solutions are expected to meet basic IP & P requirements for information being serviced or passing through the cloud solution (offering). Each cell outlines *level of fit* from the perspective of risk, cost, and evolution of use. The litmus test helps determine if the offering is a possibility.
3. If there is more than one option possible for a cell, review the cost and potential future data constraints.

Information Asset Lifecycle and Cloud Models

To round off our cloud context model, we need to incorporate information asset lifecycles for cloud services—how they are developed, deployed, distributed,

EXHIBIT 6.6 Best Fit of Cloud Type Based on IP & P and Cloud Deployment and Service Model

	Private Cloud	Hybrid Cloud	Public Cloud	Community Cloud
BPaaS	Best fit for cloud solutions dealing with information that is classified as sensitive, or organizations where the reputational impact is very significant. *Litmus test:* Does data in flight or at rest contain PII for which the other solutions cannot provide guaranteed auditability and meet constraints associated with IP & P use in a private cloud?	Use where external service providers participate in the business process but are not a part of the organization. Service providers need to meet IP & P and auditability constraints. In many cases, they will belong to a community cloud, with a trust relationship between parties. *Litmus test:* Are all services that do not operate in the private cloud carrying data that meets IP & P constraints, and are they auditable?	Normally not a fit except for read-only, non-sensitive data, normally shared in the public context. *Litmus test:* Are all services that operate in the public cloud carrying data that meets IP & P constraints, and are they auditable?	Good fit for business processes dealing with community activities—e.g., registration for a club, within a government cloud, and organizational supply chains. *Litmus test:* Can the offering meet ILM, accounting, and auditability constraints?
SaaS	Typically a poor fit where large sets of processes (e.g., CRM) are handled in the context of the cloud as a whole. Can be a good fit for specific service-oriented categories (e.g., a fill-order service) within the context of an enterprise. *Litmus Test:* Do the IP & P requirements justify a private SaaS (in terms of cost or risk)?	A combination of SaaS providers chained in a community cloud can and do exist. Good examples are common in financial services. In practical terms you can only trust your neighbor and govern him/her. *Litmus Test:* Can data that is stored or transported over	Best fit as the volumes of scale and the reuse opportunity are significant enough for the business model to typically be a good fit. SaaS providers typically encapsulate consumers from the risks of privacy and protection. *Litmus Test:* Can the cloud provider meet the IP & P	Dependent on the service type being offered, where significant data is not at risk, SaaS can be offered effectively and be a tool in a community cloud. *Litmus Test:* Can IP & P requirements be met? Can auditability and accounting controls be met?

(Continued)

115

EXHIBIT 6.6 (Continued)

	Private Cloud	Hybrid Cloud	Public Cloud	Community Cloud
SaaS (Continued)	Is there likely to be service reuse?	non-private cloud components support IP & P requirements? Is there auditability across the service chain?	requirements? What risks exist from a locality independence perspective? Is there a risk from the co-mingling of data (if there is data co-mingling)? Can integrity and confidentiality requirements be met in an acceptable and auditable manner?	
PaaS	Good fit. Same rationale as SaaS applies. *Litmus Test:* Do the IP & P requirements justify a private PaaS (in terms of cost or risk)? (In many cases, they will).	Good fit *if* organizations can take advantages of public offerings with a PaaS model (e.g., Amazon EC2) and leverage private security constraints. *Litmus Test:* Can the IP & P requirements be met in an auditable manner? Can co-mingling issues be addressed? Is there the requisite governance framework and tooling?	Average Fit. Though platforms such as Amazon's EC2 and Google's GAE product provide platforms in which to develop cloud solutions, the privacy and protection risks, and the lack of standards and interoperability prevent widespread adoption. ILM, locality independence, and multitenancy play a much larger role. *Litmus Test:* Can the IP & P requirements (in terms of cost or risk) be met, without risk to	Poor fit. Information privacy and protection constraints tend to be a limiting factor. Until standards and mechanisms to enforce them go mainstream, the possibility of adoption of community cloud PaaS solutions is limited. *Litmus Test:* Are there mechanisms in place to support auditability? Can ILM requirements be met? What are the multitenancy and location independence implications?

data? Can the ILM requirements be met? Can auditability requirements be met?

IaaS	Best Fit. IaaS solutions, offered as managed solutions by infrastructure groups in organizations, are a good fit and relatively mature. They also offer the greatest usage opportunity across large to mid-sized business and the added value of externalizing concerns on privacy and protection and making them cross cutting. Chargeback models have also matured. Issues typically occur across varying SLAs. *Litmus Test:* Does the IP & P cost and the chargeback model support multiple customers in the organization? Are the IP & P requirements sufficiently similar for a cloud solution to be a fit? Are there any regulatory issues associated with co-mingling?	Good fit, as adopting organizations can encapsulate the offerings from the public offerings with constraints that their particular business requires. Hybrid cloud solutions enable the separation management of information so that different information elements can be stored in different data stores. Key limitations revolve around location independence, multi-tenancy, and data in flight. *Litmus Test:* Do the IP & P constraints permit a hybrid cloud? Can ILM, multitenancy, and locality issues be met? Can the separation of information assets between private and public elements of the hybrid cloud be supported?	Best Fit for SMB/mid-sized businesses and scenarios without highly confidential data. The biggest issues with their adoption are integrity, multitenancy, and location independence. Performance constraints also act as a limitation. For certain scenarios (e.g., offsite backup), this can be the best fit. *Litmus Test:* Do the IP & P constraints permit a public cloud? Can ILM, integrity, multitenancy, and locality issues be met? Are there the requisite controls in place to support auditability, accounting, and information integrity?	Best Fit for organizations and individuals without highly confidential data, unless it is maintained by a reputable authority (e.g., government). In the case of supply chain style community clouds, the issue is to ensure that auditability, integrity, and ILM constraints can be verifiably implemented. *Litmus Test:* Do the IP & P constraints permit the use of a community cloud? Are there the requisite controls in place to support auditability, accounting, and information integrity?

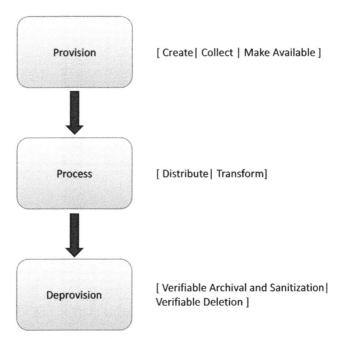

EXHIBIT 6.7 Information Lifecycle in the Context of the Cloud

transformed, and de-provisioned (verifiably archived or deleted). Each of these stages in the lifecycle of a cloud service has security and data privacy connotations. Exhibit 6.7 illustrates the different stages in the lifecycle of a cloud service, irrespective of the service model.

The Jericho Forum,[20] the SNIA,[21] and Short[22] provide a good overview of general Information Lifecycle Management (ILM) concepts and practices.

Data Privacy in the Cloud

> The personal life of every individual is based on secrecy, and perhaps it is partly for that reason that civilized man is so nervously anxious that personal privacy should be respected.
>
> —*Anton Chekov*

Data privacy in the cloud takes on more complications than traditional privacy. For example, a cloud characteristic is locality independence. However, this has implications from a data privacy context as data privacy laws vary based on locality. Thus, some mechanism to tag and audit data movement and residency becomes a necessity. In many cases, the laws are immature and evolving, sometimes through the courts establishing precedent as opposed to legislation. The implication is very clear: make sure that there is a clear and defined contractual relationship, as well as an incorporation of the temporal risk of changing data privacy requirements. Where this is not clear, consumers should err on the side of caution. A more detailed review of the legal state and standards is presented in the following section on regulatory and compliance implications.

Data Classification in the Context of the Cloud

Data classification is the basis on which an understanding of the privacy and information security implications of assets in the cloud can be established. Data classification schemes help outline security and privacy commitments; they take on greater significance in a cloud context because they help establish guidelines and a contractual basis for defining data privacy and protection responsibilities, as well as make architectural decisions. The section on standards provides a further outline on data classification schemes.

 ## REGULATORY AND COMPLIANCE IMPLICATIONS

Information protection and privacy in the context of the cloud involves addressing all elements of the security continuum, including data in flight and at rest at both the service provider and consumer level.

Standards need to be thought of in a national and international context, while taking into consideration the challenges that cloud computing brings. Because of the rapid evolution of technology, what is happening in practice is that legislation is lagging behind reality,[23] and jurisprudence is being established by precedent through case law.[24] The implications are varying opinions and a lack of clarity, which inhibits adoption and presents risk to all parties. Concerns for individual privacy due to this lack of clarity thus prohibit adoption. Standards are immature and are being defined or don't exist, or when they do exist, they do not address current issues.

Standards for privacy deal with PII, and its lifecycle in the context of the cloud (where it is stored, where it travels, etc.). Standards of importance in a national context are FERPA (Family Educational Rights and Privacy Act),[25] FAIR practices, OECD guidelines,[26] the EU Data Protection Directive,[27] and the UN's declaration of Human Rights.[28] Key issues in a cloud context are locality, multitenancy, and privacy concerns based on data classification. Locality independence is at odds with the law and safe harbor.[29] Organizations such as EPIC,[30] and industries, are addressing these issues separately within their context. For example, the health-care industry has evolving guidance for *personal health information* (PHI), and the seriousness under which this is viewed is now leading to prison terms.[31]

Data classification schemes form the basis for making privacy and protection decisions in the context of the cloud. The data classification standards space can be divided into global standards, and further divided on the basis of commercial, governmental, and intergovernmental use. In a commercial context, typical classification varies based on domain (health-care, PII, financial PII, education, etc.).[32] In the United States, in a governmental context in general, the U.S. FIPS 199[33] applies. The sharing of information between governmental organizations in the case of G-8 countries is based on the Traffic Light Protocol (TLP)[34] to show the privacy restriction level of the data. FERPA information is regulated by the Family Policy Compliance Office (FPCO). This information is built on the data classification called *Directory*. This gives consent of student information by default (student name, address, telephone, and e-mail). This government information is accessible by private industry and is the basis of most financial institutions' first contact with new customers for services (student loans, credit cards, consumer financing). The conflict in the cloud is privacy between government and financial industries. The government organization FERPA views the privacy of student information as a right that must be protected in order to ensure civil liberties of the student (Leroy Rooker versus University of Miami, June 2002). The financial industry sees privacy as a barrier to services that must be delivered in order to benefit the student or customer. The conflict over privacy in the cloud will continue to be an issue across several government and industry sectors because personal privacy is viewed as a barrier to inform and empower the customer with information that will benefit their lives by business services.

Privacy is defined as proper or appropriate use and protection of private information. Exhibit 6.8 provides a listing of key regulatory requirements and the conflict areas in the context of different business domains.

EXHIBIT 6.8 The Gap between Regulations and Business Drivers

Business Domain	Conflict	Implication
Education	FERPA vs. Financials	"Student directory used to send card application"
Health Care	HIPPA vs. Pharmacy	"Patient health record used to send drug ad"
Legal	Bar Association vs. Legal Services	"Court records used to send legal ads"
Energy	Fourth Amendment vs. Smart Grid Technology	"Home energy records used to send furnace ads"

A CLOUD INFORMATION ASSET PROTECTION AND PRIVACY PLAYBOOK

So now that we understand what a cloud means and the associated implications, what do we do about it? How do the consumer, provider, and regulator ensure Information Protection and Privacy? To address these questions, we present a playbook, which outlines steps to be taken to define a Cloud Information Protection and Privacy Specification at the level of an information security service flow.

The playbook uses the security reference model described earlier in the chapter. It provides some basic steps that an organization in one of the three types of stakeholders can undertake to assess the impact of pursuing a cloud solution. Its core principles are the "principle of atomicity" (described earlier in the security reference model), the principle that "the scope and level of protection should be specific and appropriate to the asset at risk,"[35] and the principle that you "assume context at your peril."[36]

The approach we recommend is to address information protection and privacy in the context of *each link (security element)* in the *chain (security service flow)* separately. A link further down the chain is obligated to meet the information privacy and protection constraints defined for that particular atomic security element, and the overall particular security service flow identified in the Cloud Information Privacy and Protection Specification (the Specification). The assurance requirements in the Specification provide the ability to validate compliance at each step, thus ensuring adequate coverage of security for the entire service flow. The playbook recommends that the definition of the information lifecycle for information assets associated within the flow is done, and that state transitions are verifiable. This needs to be clearly defined and be contractually and practically enforceable, accompanied by a policy for consistent auditing for compliance and be available in the Specification.

The value of this approach is that we can define the specific information protection guidelines for each link in the chain separately, reducing the process of addressing the information protection and privacy of a flow to one element at a time. This approach also allows us to separate out infrastructural decisions and standards, facilitating interoperability and keeping the problem domain simple. The playbook uses Exhibit 6.7 to define behaviors of cloud models based on deployment type and service models. These are further qualified by characteristic, line of business (e.g., finance, health care, etc.), and then by the type of data that is going to be stored. Finally, the user should incorporate the impact of the temporal and location independence aspects of the data.

The steps are:

1. Define the Base Information (Data) Protection and Privacy Policy Set.
   a. Define the kind of data
      i. What kinds of data are involved?
         1. Classify the data and create a set of policies by data class.
      ii. What is its lifecycle? For each of the categories of data, define a lifecycle specification.
         2. Update the Information Protection Policies.
   b. Determine the line of business.
      i. What are the special legal and compliance requirements of the line of business?
         1. How do they apply to the different data classes?
      ii. Update the Information Protection Policies.
   c. Determine the temporal nature of the data.
      i. Can it change its meaning over time?
      ii. Do compliance implications have an impact?
      iii. Update the Data Policies.
2. Define the security continuum context for the cloud solution.
   The *security continuum context* is a combination of the service chain/ flow involved, the data that will flow through the chain, the functional nature of the end service being provided to the end consumer, and the policies associated with that data.
   a. Define the context for the overall solution.
   b. Next, define the context in terms of an atomic security continuum element.
      i. For each atomic security element:

1. Apply the data classification scheme and the Confidentiality, Integrity, Availability, Authentication, Authorization, Accounting, and Audit (CIAAAAA) to arrive at the information protection and privacy requirements.
2. Apply this to data at rest and data in flight.
3. Update the Information Protection and Privacy Policies.
3. Create a security solution specification.

The end result of this will be an Information Protection and Privacy Policy set, architecture, technology, audit, and risk blueprint. *We believe that it is important to externalize audit in the context of the cloud and to define clear standards, so that all three stakeholders can use the same data and have clear expectations.* It will be composed of the sum of all security service flows involved in the solution architecture.

The resulting deliverables for each security service flow will form a part of the *Cloud Information Protection and Privacy Specification* (the Specification)—see Exhibit 6.9. It will be composed of:

a. An Information Policy Specification
b. An Information Standards Taxonomy to be satisfied for each atomic element.

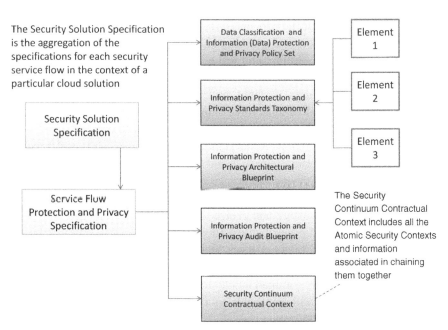

EXHIBIT 6.9 The Cloud Information Protection and Privacy Solution Specification

   c. An Architectural Blueprint, including a set of architectural decisions which helps define the infrastructure for the atomic element.

   d. An Audit Blueprint, which specifies what will be collected, and when.

   e. A Security Continuum Contractual Context, including the set of contractual obligations and specifications that must be then met for each of the atomic elements. In many cases, these contractual commitments may be daisy-chained with the service provider in each case being obligated to comply with the specific requirements for the service flow.

IN SUMMARY

> For tomorrow belongs to the people who prepare for it today.
>
> —*African proverb*

Cloud computing and its rapid adoption is changing the very way we think about Information Protection and Privacy. To be able to prepare for and deal with it, we believe that the concept of the atomic security element, involving the consumer, provider, and regulator should provide the basis for a mechanism to view a cloud solution, and will get formalized in the form of standard usage models.

The concept of data in flight and rest are already expressed in the Collaboration Oriented Architecture,[37] and we believe they will gain greater importance as consumers and providers strive to achieve integrity, confidentiality, and non-repudiation. Audit standards and requirements will become more important, with the ability to define interoperable audit specifications for data elements, with varying privacy guidelines based on data classification, lifecycle, and locality becoming defining attributes of sustained, successful cloud solutions. Technology will evolve to support the capabilities needed to ensure protection and privacy across the continuum.

Examples include ongoing work at the Open Group to define a cloud reference architecture and cloud security architecture, the emerging cloud audit standard,[38] early commercial offerings,[39] work on privacy preservation for public content,[40] and searchable encryption.[41] Research also shows that consumers *desire and will expect* the same privacy and protection in the virtual world that they get within the physical world.[42]

Finally, privacy laws and their interpretation will need to evolve to address concerns of the limitations of notice and choice.[43] Currently, case law is driving the jurisprudence and that will need to evolve so that legislation drives it, providing a more consistent and predictable platform. The other thing to consider is the evolution of safe harbor provisions and the concept that data on the cloud is entitled to the same protection and privacy provisions as data in the consumer's residence or place of work. Commercial organizations have started adopting the Traffic Light Protocol approach to transcend international and organizational boundaries.[44] What is PII will evolve.[45] Cloud providers will become custodians of the data and will be required to mitigate issues associated with residence/locality, access, auditability, confidentiality, and integrity.

NOTES

1. J. Soat, The Cloud's Five Biggest Weaknesses, www.informationweek.com/cloud-computing/blog/archives/2010/06/the_clouds_five.html (accessed June 12, 2010). WSJ. "China, Google and the Cloud Wars: Your Personal Sata Still Aren't Safe." Retrieved May 12, 2010, from the *Wall Street Journal* (January 22, 2010), http://online.wsj.com/article/SB10001424052748703699204575501680150 1346056.html.
2. T. G. Peter Mell, The NIST Definition of Cloud Computing, V15, NIST (2009).
3. N. Kumar, Understanding the Role of Security in SOA and Cloud Computing. Proceedings of the 1st Security Practitioners Conference (San Diego, CA: The Open Group, February, 2009).
4. CDT, CDT Comments on U.S. Department of Commerce Information Privacy and Innovation. Information Privacy and Innovation Docket No. 100402174017501 (USA: Center for Democracy and Technology, June 14, 2010).
5. Privacy Rights Clearinghouse, Chronology of Data Breaches (June 18, 2010), www .privacyrights.org/ar/chrondatabreaches.htm (accessed June 18, 2010).
6. EPIC, Cloud Computing, http://epic.org/privacy/cloudcomputing/ (accessed June 11, 2010).
7. T. Forsheit, What a Farming Bankruptcy Can Teach Us About Privacy in the Cloud, http://www.infolawgroup.com/2010/06/articles/cloud-computing-1/what-a-farming-bankruptcy-can-teach-us-about-privacy-in-the-cloud/ (accessed June 2, 2010).
8. T. G. Peter Mell, The NIST Definition of Cloud Computing, V15, NIST (2009).
9. Service Oriented Architecture : What Is SOA? (The Open Group, April 2009), www.opengroup.org/soa/source-book/soa/soa.htm (accessed May 18, 2010).
10. T. G. Peter Mell, The NIST Definition of Cloud Computing, V15, NIST (2009).
11. Ibid.

12. Ibid.

13. Gartner Newsroom. Gartner Highlights Five Attributes of Cloud Computing (June 23, 2009), www.gartner.com/it/page.jsp?id=1035013 (accessed May 21, 2010).

14. P. Wainewright, Many Degrees of Multi-Tenancy (June 16, 2008), www.zdnet .com/blog/saas/many-degrees-of-multi-tenancy/533 (accessed June 20, 2010). Frederick Chong, G. C. (June 2006). Multi-Tenant Data Architecture. Retrieved June 05, 2010, from MSDN: http://msdn.microsoft.com/en-us/ library/aa479086.aspx.

15. Jericho Forum, Position Paper Collaboration Oriented Architectures, Version 1.0 (The Open Group, 2008).

16. N. Kumar, *The New World in this Ecomomy: The Role of SOA, Cloud Computing, Saas & Web 2.0 in Business Optimization & Alignment.* Optimization & Alignment Strategies Seminar. Chicago, IL, USA: Technology Executive Club, March 19, 2009).

17. K. Lieberherr, I. Holland, A. Riel, "Object-Oriented Programming: An Objective Sense of Style." *OOPSLA* (San Diego, CA: ACM, 1988): 323–334.

18. D. Juan, W. Wei, X. Gu, and T. Yu, "Towards Secure DataFlow Processing in Open Systems," STC'09 (Chicago: ACM, 2009).

19. Jericho Forum, Jericho Forum™ Commandments (The Open Group, 2007).

20. Jericho Forum, Information Lifecycle Management, Version 1.0, (The Open Group, 2009).

21. SNIA, Information Life Cycle Management Roadmap. Data Management Forum of the Storage Network industry Association (2004).

22. J. Short, Information Lifecycle Management Concepts, Practices, and Value (San Diego, CA: Society for Information Management, Advanced Practices Council, 2007).

23. P. Meller "Microsoft's Top Lawyer Urges New EU Laws for Cloud Computing" (January 26, 2010), www.computerworld.com/s/article/9149038/Microsoft_s_ top_lawyer_urges_new_EU_laws_for_cloud_computing (accessed May 10, 2010). R. Gellman, Privacy in the Clouds: Risks to Privacy and Confidentiality from Cloud Computing, World Privacy Forum (2009).

24. T. Forsheit, What a Farming Bankruptcy Can Teach Us About Privacy in the Cloud, www.infolawgroup.com/2010/06/articles/cloud-computing-1/what-a-farming-bankruptcy-can-teach-us-about-privacy-in-the-cloud/ (accessed June 2, 2010). Goldman, E., 9th Circuit Affirms Rejection of Data Breach Claims Against Gap—Ruiz v. Gap. Retrieved June 06, 2010, from Technology & Marketing Law Blog: http://blog.ericgoldman.org/archives/2010/06/9th_ circuit_aff.htm. Lemos, R. (Aprill 22, 2009). When the FBI Raids a Data Center: A Rare Danger. Retrieved May 15, 2010, from NetworkWorld: www. network world.com/news/2009/042209-when-the-fbi-raids-a.html. Rothken,

I. P. E-DISCOVERY 2.0. Retrieved June 10, 2010, from California Lawyer: www .callawyer.com/story.cfm?eid=909892&evid=1.

25. Federal Trade Commission, Fair Information Practice Principles (June 25, 2007), www.ftc.gov/reports/privacy3/fairinfo.shtm (accessed June 5, 2010).

26. OECD, OECD Guidelines on the Protection of Privacy and Transborder Flows of Personal Data (September 23, 1980), www.oecd.org/document/18/ 0,3343,en_2649_34255_1815186_1_1_1_1,00.html (accessed June 3, 2010).

27. European Union, Data Protection (n.d.), http://ec.europa.eu/justice_home/fsj/ privacy/index_en.htm (accessed May 10, 2010).

28. United Nations, The Universal Declaration of Human Rights (December 10, 1948), www.un.org/en/documents/udhr/ (accessed May 15, 2010).

29. ITA-ECTF, Safe Harbor Privacy Principles, etc. (U.S. Department of Commerce Electronic Commerce Task Force, 2000), www.ita.doc.gov/td/ecom/menu. html (accessed May 20, 2010). FTC. (n.d.). Safe Harbor Overview. Retrieved May 20, 2010, from Safe Harbor Framework: www.export.gov/safeharbor/ index.asp.

30. EPIC (n.d.), http://epic.org/privacy/cloudcomputing/google/#complaint.

31. HDM, Prison for HIPAA Privacy Violator (April 28, 2010), www.healthdata management.com/news/hipaa_privacy-violation-conviction-breach-40202-1 .html (accessed May 23, 2010).

32. D. Shackelford, Regulations and Standards: Where Encryption Applies, SANS (2007). Markham, B. (2008, February 29). Data Classification and Privacy: A Foundation for Compliance. A Workshop on Data Privacy for Maryland Higher Education. College Park: University of Maryland.

33. FIPS, Standards for Security Categorization of Federal Information and Information Systems, National Institute of Standards and Technology, Federal Information Processing Standards Publication (Gaithersburg: U.S. Department of Commerce, 2004).

34. ENISA, Info Handling: Information Handling Improvement (2010), www .enisa.europa.eu/act/cert/background/coop/ideas-for-future/recommendations/ info-handling (accessed May 25, 2010).

35. Jericho Forum, Jericho Forum™ Commandments (The Open Group, 2007).

36. Ibid.

37. The Jericho Forum, Position Paper Collaboration Oriented Architectures, Version 1.0 (The Open Group, 2008).

38. CloudAudit, A6—The Automated Audit, Assertion, Assessment, and Assurance API (2010), www.cloudaudit.org/ (accessed June 5, 2010).

39. M. Ricknäs, Amazon encrypts CloudFront, but security comes at a price (June 9, 2010), www.computerworld.com.au/article/349318/amazon_encrypts_ cloudfront_security_comes_price/ (accessed June 11, 2010).

40. E. Bertino, M. Nabell , N. Shang, and J. Zage, Mask: A System for Privacy-Preserving Policy-Based Access to Published Content. Proceedings of the 2010 international conference on Management of data Indianapolis: ACM, 2010), 1239–1242).

41. Q. C. Jin Li, Fuzzy Keyword Search over Encrypted Data in Cloud Computing. INFOCOM 2010, Proceedings IEEE (San Diego, CA: IEEE, 2010), 1–5.

42. Zogby International, Results from June 4–7 Nationwide Poll. (Zogby International, 2010).

43. L. Shinn, CDT Submits Comments to European Commission on Privacy (January 6, 2010), www.cdt.org/blogs/lindsey-shinn/cdt-submits-comments-european-commission-privacy (accessed May 18, 2010).

44. *Information Security Magazine* (July 2008.) "Interview: CISO Adrian Seccombe on Eli Lilly from FIPCO to FIPNET," http://searchsecurity.techtarget.com/magazineFeature/0,296894,sid14_gci1321717,00.html (accessed May 18, 2010).

45. CDT, Comments of the Center for Democracy & Technology on the Staff Discussion Draft of the Consumer Privacy Legislation (USA: Center for Democracy & Technology, 2010).

CHAPTER SEVEN

Business Continuity and Disaster Recovery

Jeff Fenton

T HIS CHAPTER COVERS Business Continuity Planning (BCP) and Disaster Recovery Planning (DRP) considerations for cloud computing. The first section covers the main points of BCP and DRP as they apply to all environments. These points apply whether or not the organization is utilizing cloud computing services. The second section presents options for using cloud services to augment or replace traditional disaster recovery strategies. The third section introduces the new issues to include in DRP when using cloud services. Each section includes key points for auditors to emphasize when assessing an organization's BCP and DRP posture.

BUSINESS CONTINUITY PLANNING AND DISASTER RECOVERY PLANNING OVERVIEW

This section outlines the basic concepts of BCP and DRP. These concepts, including audit considerations, apply to all environments, whether on-premises or cloud-based.

Problem Statement

The purpose of BCP is to enable an organization to withstand a disruptive event and continue in business. In BCP, the organization must identify its critical business deliverables—the products and services it sells—and the business processes and resources (especially people, facilities, and equipment) that enable producing these deliverables. The organization must also identify the dependencies among its critical business processes and its dependencies on business partners such as suppliers. The first point to emphasize is to think of the business first. Once the organization has taken these steps, it can then identify the computing, network, and information resources that support its critical processes. This activity, Disaster Recovery Planning (DRP), follows completing the business continuity plan. Thus, the disaster recovery plan is a component of an overall hierarchy of plans. The business continuity plan is at the top of the hierarchy, with the disaster recovery plan and other plans (emergency response, crisis management, crisis communication) as components.

Senior executive support is critical for success in BCP and DRP. Senior management should express its commitment to perform these activities as part of managing risk for the organization. The impact of a disruption can include loss of reputation, loss of shareholder value, and legal and regulatory consequences that could greatly exceed the actual value of lost production or lost sales. The BCP and DRP are the keys to managing this risk. A good business continuity plan enables the organization to anticipate and mitigate many specific risks before a disruptive event happens, and respond more effectively after an event to mitigate the impact. The organization should have written policies requiring BCP and DRP activities. An executive champion should communicate in writing to support the BCP and DRP teams to help them gain the support and cooperation of stakeholders across the organization.

BCP and DRP activities should be performed as a formal project, with a project manager and a cross-functional team. An organization may appoint an individual as a BCP and/or DRP coordinator to provide technical leadership. Smaller organizations may consider utilizing a consultant in this role during the initial development, testing, and training of the plans. Other team participants should include engineering, research and development, marketing, supply chain management, and manufacturing, along with supporting organizations such as human resources, legal counsel, facilities, safety, security, public relations, and information technology (IT). If the organization structure includes program manager roles for key deliverables, the team should include program representatives. An organization with multiple sites should include site representatives. If the organization has an emergency management or crisis management specialist or team, that function should also be included in the BCP team.

The Planning Process

The phases of BCP include:

- **Initiation:** gaining senior management support, forming the team, scoping and planning the project, identifying critical products and services, identifying critical business processes and facilities, and identifying critical internal and external business-level dependencies such as suppliers.
- **Risk Assessment:** identifying the relevant disruption threats and vulnerabilities, including information security threats and health threats to personnel.
- **Business Impact Analysis:** identifying the length of disruption that can be tolerated for critical deliverables and the tolerable outage time for key business processes, and identifying the scenarios by which threats can impact the business, such as the impact on manufacturing if a major supplier is unable to deliver parts, the impact of a flood on a particular facility and the rest of the organization, or a utility outage. Neighboring community events that do not impact a facility directly, such as an outside gas release requiring people to remain in place, should also be considered.
- **Business Continuity Strategy:** identifying alternative resources required to restore critical processes such as an alternate facility or alternate suppliers, and recommending and implementing countermeasures to mitigate risks in advance of a disruptive event, for example, an uninterrupted power supply (UPS) generator. Note that in the initial phase of recovery, business processes would probably be recoverable to some fraction of normal capacity, especially at an alternate facility.
- **Business Continuity Plan Documentation:** writing the plan(s) to implement the selected strategy, covering response team roles and responsibilities, assessing damage and determining whether to activate all or part(s) of the plan(s), activation process, communicating with stakeholders (including employees, non-employees, customers, suppliers, investors, news media, and public authorities), response procedures, recovery procedures, and restoration procedures to return to normal

production. This phase should also include establishing needed relationships before an event takes place, such as contracting with alternate suppliers and having the appropriate individuals become acquainted with local news media and public authorities. The recovery procedures must include the alternate facilities and resources required; the specific systems and applications to be recovered; step-by-step instructions to perform the recovery in order of priority; and the individuals authorized to contact recovery site vendors, offsite media storage vendors, and other suppliers designated in the plan. The plan(s) should also include a process for tracking the status of response and recovery activities and maintaining situational awareness, especially in the early emergency phase.

▪ **Business Continuity Plan Testing:** drills and exercises to validate the plan(s) and the participants' readiness to execute them. Exercises may range from discussion or tabletop exercises (role play) through drills (simulated events) to full-scale exercises. Testing activities should include setting the scope, objectives, scenarios, and timelines for tests; recording results and lessons learned; and following up on all areas for improvement.

▪ **Business Continuity Awareness and Training:** training all plan participants in their respective roles and providing awareness training for all populations of employees and non-employees in the site(s) and business units covered by the plan(s).

▪ **Business Continuity Plan Maintenance:** updating the plan(s) to incorporate changes in business needs and processes, evolving threats and vulnerabilities, and changes in team participants; and communicating the updated plan(s).

The phases of DRP are similar, with the emphasis on computing and information resources that enable the critical business processes, including voice and data networks. The two major considerations for timeliness in recovering IT resources must be based on the Business Impact Analysis (BIA):

1. **Recovery Time Objective (RTO):** the earliest point when an IT system, network, or application must be made available to support critical business processes.

2. **Recovery Point Objective (RPO):** the point to which data must be current when an IT resource is recovered. For example, if it is acceptable to recover with data up to one week old, the RPO would be seven days.

As with business processes, the initial recovery phase in a disaster recovery plan would probably include recovering IT resources to a fraction of their normal capacity, especially when an alternate data center and other alternative arrangements are involved. Traditionally, strategies for IT recovery have included redundant data centers, real-time remote backup or transaction logging, *hot* sites (vendor-provided recovery data centers with compatible computer hardware but requiring installing software and restoring data from backup media after a disruption), *warm* or *cold* sites (alternate facilities without computers and possibly without peripheral and network hardware), and offsite storage vendors (for tapes and other backup media). For DRP, the systems and applications must be identified for recovery in order of priority.

The Auditor's Role

The auditor's role is to assess the organization's planning process and verify that plans cover the needed scope, are comprehensive, and are tested. The outcome of an audit should be an indicator of the organization's preparedness to withstand the types of disruptions that can reasonably be anticipated. The audit should include the following questions:[1]

- Who is responsible to lead BCP and DRP activities?
- Are all plans current, and are all copies current?
- Does the BCP identify critical business deliverables to customers and the tolerable outage or delay times for deliverables?
- Does the BCP identify critical business functions that support the deliverables?
- Are dependencies among critical business functions, and dependencies on external partners, identified?
- Have critical facilities and equipment been identified? Are there plans to relocate the needed number of end users to alternate workspace?
- Have critical human resources been identified?
- Does the BCP identify the threats, vulnerabilities, and disruption scenarios relevant to the business processes and facilities involved? Are scenarios with warning (such as a hurricane watch) included along with sudden-onset scenarios such as an earthquake? Are information security incidents and health incidents (pandemic) included?
- Contact a selection of response and recovery team members. Do the participants understand their roles and responsibilities?
- Have IT systems and applications been identified for their priority, RTO, and RPO?

- Has the needed capacity for each IT system been identified in recovery mode, for example, by percentage of normal production capacity, number of concurrent users, or number of transactions per second? Have recovery system configurations been sized to support required capacities?
- Are routine data backup procedures consistent with the RPO for each respective application?
- Is there a damage assessment process to determine whether a disruption is sufficiently serious to activate business continuity and disaster recovery plans?
- Ask members of the recovery team to step through the instructions for recovering selected systems and applications.
- Are telecommunication networks and systems identified with instructions for their recovery and restoration? Are arrangements documented for telephone service at alternate facilities? Can incoming calls be rerouted?
- Are procedures to move to a new facility, or to restore the existing damaged facility, documented? Will a separate team work in parallel on restoration to enable recovery teams to concentrate on recovery? Do the restoration procedures include testing restored systems in parallel while recovery systems are still running?
- How recently were BCP and DR exercises conducted? Were objectives identified for each exercise, results documented, and lessons learned followed up?
- Are all expected media at the offsite media storage vendor, and are all media properly labeled? Is the inventory updated when media are shipped offsite and received back at the production site?
- If backup data media are encrypted, how does the organization manage the encryption keys? Who is authorized to have access to encryption keys?
- Evaluate the physical security, safety, environmental controls, and electrical power arrangements at the recovery data center and offsite media storage vendor.
- Evaluate the equipment at the recovery data center. Is all equipment covered in the contract present in the required configurations? Are firmware and software up to date? Are operating system versions as specified in the DR plan?
- Does the DR plan include provisions for transferring software licenses to a recovery computer, or obtaining temporary licenses?
- Does the DR plan document the arrangements for information security in a recovery data center environment, including firewall and router

configurations, authentication, access control to systems and applications, and wiping data media after a recovery test or actual recovery?

- Are the designated individuals allowed to contact the recovery data center and offsite storage vendor pre-arranged and is the list up to date? Will the vendors accept calls only from these individuals?

- What are the provisions in the recovery data center contract, when the vendor's primary site is fully utilized by other customers at the time the organization needs access to recover from a disaster?

- How will stakeholders be informed of the status of recovery and restoration, including employees, non-employees, suppliers, customers, and investors? Are all employees and non-employees required to refer news media inquiries to a public relations professional? Are there arrangements to hold a news conference, at an alternate location if needed?

AUGMENTING TRADITIONAL DISASTER RECOVERY WITH CLOUD SERVICES

For organizations with IT on premises, cloud computing services can augment or replace traditional DR strategies by providing a remotely accessible, distributed architecture.[2] Whereas traditional DR options might preclude a real-time recovery strategy because of the cost of dedicated computer platforms and storage, a cloud service could make real-time recovery a realistic option. Similarly, Infrastructure as a Service (IaaS) providers can offer flexible access to compatible computer platforms replacing the traditional hot site option, putting real-time recovery within the reach of more organizations. An organization could utilize an IaaS provider in the role of a hot site in its DR plan (activating the capability only after a disruptive event occurs, perhaps still physically shipping backup media), or in real time simultaneously with normal production. The organization might mix the options, utilizing IaaS for storage while still using a traditional hot site for computer platforms. Even with a traditional hot site, this arrangement would achieve a more rapid RTO by eliminating the time for physically shipping media. Arranging for IaaS services is usually simpler and faster than contracting with a traditional hot site vendor.

The ubiquity of cloud computing services is another key advantage. While a traditional hot site vendor might only offer one or a few sites requiring dedicated network connectivity, a cloud provider could offer multiple sites easily accessible across the Internet.[3] This advantage can also make alternate workspace arrangements more flexible. Users might sit at the alternate workspace but would access the cloud provider through a web browser instead of needing dedicated connectivity from the alternate workspace to a hot site. Some IaaS providers offer hybrid architectures with an appliance at an organization's premises that performs backups to a cloud storage service.

IaaS storage and computing platform providers can also reduce the oversubscription risk involved with a hot site vendor. Traditional hot site subscriptions are typically geographically specific; that is, a customer organization will contract to utilize a particular site the vendor provides. The vendor might offer an alternate site if the primary site is oversubscribed with customers, which could occur in an area-wide disaster affecting many organizations. With a cloud-based strategy, the customer would not be tied to a specific hot site location.

CLOUD COMPUTING AND DISASTER RECOVERY: NEW ISSUES TO CONSIDER

When utilizing cloud services for disaster recovery or as part of production IT strategy, an organization will face several new issues. Most importantly, the organization must consider the resiliency of the cloud provider(s) as distinguished from the resiliency of on-premises systems under the organization's control.

Cloud Computing Continuity

When an organization moves to cloud computing, whether to augment a traditional DR plan or as its primary overall IT strategy, new issues come into play involving the nature of cloud services and vendor relationships. These issues include:[4]

- Service interruption risk because of outages at the cloud provider
- Risk of data loss due to events at the cloud provider
- Vendor relationships and service level agreements (SLAs)
- Geographic location of cloud provider storage and processing, with attendant legal/regulatory and contractual issues such as privacy, electronic discovery, and payment card industry (PCI) compliance
- Vendor lock-in

- Vendor viability (what if the cloud vendor ceases business or stops providing a service?)
- Portability across cloud providers
- Integrating multiple cloud providers to reduce outage risk

These issues apply to all cloud provider models—Platform as a Service (PaaS), and Software as a Service (SaaS)[5]—though the issues of vendor lock-in, portability across cloud vendors, and integrating multiple cloud providers are most difficult for the PaaS and SaaS models. In addition, when an organization is utilizing PaaS or SaaS providers, it is more likely that the cloud is central to the organization's entire production IT strategy rather than a resource for backup and recovery.

To address these issues, the Cloud Security Alliance[6] recommends several steps, including:

- Customer organizations conducting on-site inspections of cloud providers
- Customer reviews of cloud providers for senior management support of BCP and DRP and reviews of provider business continuity and DR plans
- Customer reviews of cloud provider architectures for redundancy
- Customers going through their own BCP and DRP processes thoroughly and understanding their RTO and RPO needs before evaluating and engaging cloud providers
- Contract and SLA negotiations including defined SLAs based on customer RTO and RPO needs
- Provider certification under BCP standards such as BS 25999[7] or NFPA 1600[8]

The Cloud Security Alliance has also published a Controls Matrix[9] with recommended security controls. The controls relating to BCP and DRP at the cloud provider include:

- Having a resiliency management program
- Performing a comprehensive impact analysis
- Having a comprehensive business continuity plan in place
- Conducting business continuity tests on a regular basis
- Protecting equipment from environmental risks
- Locating equipment away from environmental threats and providing redundant equipment separated by a sufficient distance
- Protecting equipment from power and telecommunications provider outages

Audit Points to Emphasize

When assessing the BCP and DRP posture of organizations that utilize cloud computing, auditors should consider the above issues in preparing their audit questions. Auditors should also ask:

- Is the cloud provider's DR plan testable? Can the provider demonstrate failover or demonstrate a test of its DR plan without impacting other customers?
- Could the customer organization retrieve its data and move to another cloud provider after its primary cloud provider has suffered a disruption? Are there scenarios in which a primary SaaS provider could suffer an application outage but the customer's data would still be accessible? Should the customer organization consider arranging to back up data with another cloud provider before an SaaS provider suffers an outage? Is this possible—would the SaaS provider make data files available to the customer in a form that would allow backup at another (SaaS or perhaps IaaS) provider?
- Could the customer organization retrieve its data if its cloud provider has ceased business or ceased providing a specific offering?
- Has the customer implemented a virtual machine replication process[10] to facilitate moving virtual platforms from one IaaS provider to another?
- Does the customer have the right to audit and physically inspect the cloud provider?
- Can the customer specify the geographic location(s) where the cloud provider stores and processes data, or at least specify that data will be confined to a particular country or countries?
- Can the customer require that the cloud provider inform the customer if it receives any subpoena or other legal process that could impact the customer's data? If the provider must respond to a subpoena or support an investigation involving another customer's data, is there any scenario in which the customer could be impacted?[11]
- Can the customer specify that the cloud provider store logs, pertaining to any aspect of the customer's operation, within particular countries?
- Does the cloud provider offer defined redundancy options, such as the ability for the customer to replicate data in different zones within the provider's architecture?[12]
- If the customer should need to change providers, would the original provider commit to sanitizing its environment of the customer's data?[13]

- What would happen if a cloud provider is acquired by a direct competitor to the customer?[14] Would the customer be able to change providers and receive its data back?
- Can the cloud provider's sanitization of data be independently verified?[15]
- When a cloud provider has failover, is security at its secondary site(s) comparable to its primary site?[16]

IN SUMMARY

This chapter has introduced the key concepts and audit issues for Business Continuity Planning and Disaster Recovery Planning for all environments, the role of cloud services as a Disaster Recovery option, and special considerations for BCP and DRP in a cloud environment.

NOTES

1. Information Systems Audit and Control Association (ISACA), *Certified Information System Auditor (CISA) Review Manual 2007* (Rolling Meadows, IL: ISACA, 2007), 441–472.
2. Ronald L. Krutz and Russell Dean Vines, *Cloud Security: A Comprehensive Guide to Secure Cloud Computing* (Hoboken, NJ: John Wiley & Sons, 2010), 119.
3. David Linthicum, "Leveraging Cloud Computing for Business Continuity," *Disaster Recovery Journal* 23:3 (2010): 28–30.
4. Drue, Reeves and Jack Santos, *The Dark Side of Cloud Computing*. Burton Group research report. Midvale, UT: Burton Group, 2010), 1–8.
5. Drue Reeves, et al., *Cloud Computing: Transforming IT*. Burton Group research report (2009), (Midvale, UT: Burton Group, 2009), 9.
6. Cloud Security Alliance, *Security Guidance for Critical Areas of Focus in Cloud Computing, Version 2.1* (2009), 50–51.
7. British Standards Institute, BS 25999-1: 2006 Business Continuity Management.
8. National Fire Protection Association, NFPA Standard 1600: Standard on Disaster/Emergency Management and Business Continuity Programs (Quincy, MA: NFPA, 2007), www.nfpa.org/assets/files/pdf/nfpa1600.pdf (accessed August 25, 2010).
9. Cloud Security Alliance, Cloud Computing Security Controls Matrix, Version 1.1 (2010), www.cloudsecurityalliance.org/Research.html (accessed March 21, 2011), rows 78–85.

10. Kim S. Nash, Disaster Recovery in the Cloud Yields ROI (2010), www .networkworld.com/news/2010/061610-disaster-recovery-in-the-cloud.html (accessed June 24, 2010), 2.

11. Seyfarth Shaw LLP, Issues Related to Cloud Computing Arrangements (2009), www.lexology.com/library/detail.aspx?g=18052d9d-c3e7-45b5-a6f5-425fdf 672ce7 (accessed August 16, 2010), 1–2

12. Mary Brandel, "Cloud Security: Tools and Experiences," *CSO Magazine* 9:5 (2010): 14–17.

13. Chenxi Wang: A Close Look at Cloud Computing Security Issues (2010), www.csoonline.com/article/496388/forrester-a-close-look-at-cloud-computing-security-issues (accessed March 21, 2011), 2.

14. Bruce Schneier, Cloud Computing (2009), www.schneier.com/blog/archives/ 2009/06/cloud_computing.html (accessed June 30, 2010), 1.

15. Christopher Perry, *Security for Cloud Computing*, U.S. Department of the Navy Chief Information Officer report (2010), www.doncio.navy.mil/PrintView .aspx?ID=1744 (accessed June 30, 2010), 3.

16. Cloud Security Basics: Disaster Recovery and Audit Capabilities, www.hub-span.com/cloud-security/cloud-security-basics-disaster-recovery-and-audit-capabilities (accessed June 30, 2010), 2.

REFERENCES

Badger, Lee, and Tim Grance. 2010. "Standards Acceleration to Jumpstart Adoption of Cloud Computing (SAJACC)." Presentation at the National Institute of Standards and Technology [NIST] Cloud Computing Workshop, May 20, 2010. Washington, DC: NIST. http://csrc.nist.gov/groups/SNS/cloud-computing/ index.html (accessed August 16, 2010).

Blackley, Bob. 2009. "Data Availability in the Cloud." Burton Group research report. Midvale, UT: Burton Group.

Blum, Dan. 2009. "Cloud Computing Security in the Enterprise." Burton Group research report. Midvale, UT: Burton Group.

Blum, Dan. 2010. "Developing a Cloud Computing Security Strategy." Burton Group research report. Midvale, UT: Burton Group.

Brodkin, Jon. 2008. Gartner: Seven Cloud-Computing Security Risks. www .infoworld.com/print/36853 (accessed June 30, 2010).

Burton, Andrew. 2010. Cloud Backup Neglects Recovery and Security Necessary for True Cloud Disaster Recovery. http://searchdisasterrecovery.techtarget .com/generic/0,295582,sid190_gci1378775_mem1,00.html (accessed June 30, 2010).

Hathaway, Melissa. 2010. Beyond Availability: Melissa Hathaway on the Cloud. http://belfercenter.ksg.harvard.edu/publication/20250/beyond_availability.

html?breadcrumb=%2Fexperts%2F2132%2Fmelissa_hathaway (accessed August 16, 2010).

Higgins, Kelly Jackson. 2009. The 6 Worst Cloud Security Mistakes. www .darkreading.com/securityservices/security/management/showArticle.jhtml? articleID=217702062&queryText=The+6+Worst+Cloud (accessed August 16, 2010).

Information Systems Audit and Control Association (ISACA). 2010. 2010 CISA Review Course, Chapter 6: Business Continuity and Disaster Recovery (presentation slides). Rolling Meadows, IL: ISACA.

Mell, Peter, and Tim Grance. 2009. "Effectively and Securely Using the Cloud Computing Paradigm." Presentation at the National Institute of Standards and Technology [NIST] Cloud Computing Workshop, May 20, 2010. Washington, DC: NIST. http://csrc.nist.gov/groups/SNS/cloud-computing/index.html (accessed August 16, 2010).

Nicholson, John L., and Wayne C. Matus. 2009. "Choosing a Safe Path to the Clouds." Pillsbury Winthrop Shaw Pittman LLP report. www.lexology.com/library/detail .aspx?g=8abcddc4-d3ae-4fc4-a7ff-716ac3893dee (accessed August 16, 2010).

Reeves, Drue. 2010. "Building a Solid Cloud Adoption Strategy: Success by Design." Burton Group research report. Midvale, UT: Burton Group.

Reeves, Drue. 2010. "Cloud Computing Tiered Architecture." Burton Group Reference Architecture Template. Midvale, UT: Burton Group.

Simon, Norman C., Samantha V. Ettari, and Brendan M. Schulman. 2010. "Cloud Computing: Opportunities and Concerns." Kramer Levin Naftalis & Frankel LLP report. www.lexology.com/library/detail.aspx?g=91783e55-7831-405c-8a11-a2531ce93b18 (accessed August 10, 2010).

Stokes, Jon. 2010. Will the Cloud Have its Own Deepwater Horizon Disaster? http:// arstechnica.com/business/inside-the-cloud/2010/06/will-the-cloud-will-have-its-own-deepwater-horizon-disaster.ars (accessed June 30, 2010).

Tower-Pierce, Julie. 2010. Cloud Computing Legal Issues. http://searchsecurity .techtarget.com/magazineFeature/0,296894,sid14_gci1506966_mem1,00. html (accessed August 16, 2010).

Westervelt, Robert. 2009. Researchers Say Search, Seizure Protection May Not Apply to SaaS Data. http://searchsecurity.techtarget.com/news/article/0,289142, sid14_gci1363283_mem1,00.html (accessed August 16, 2010).

Whittaker, Zack. 2008. What Possible Computer Disasters Can Be Associated with Cloud Computing? http://knol.google.com/k/what-possible-computer-disasters-can-be-associated-with-cloud-computing (accessed June 30, 2010).

CHAPTER EIGHT

Global Regulation and Cloud Computing

Jeremy Rissi
Sean Sherman

C LOUD COMPUTING IS many things, ranging from an exciting new business model to merely refining an old and existing technology. This chapter does not attempt to define cloud computing. It instead focuses on the relationship of cloud computing and regulation, defines the causes and impact of regulation, and tries to predict what future regulation may look like. A company or agency planning to leverage cloud computing or preparing for market, customer, or auditor oversight of a cloud computing implementation must answer practical questions such as: *What are regulatory issues I should examine?* and *What is the real effect of regulation?*

Because cloud computing is still early in its adoption cycle, there are many service providers in the marketplace, many options regarding implementation, and not yet many rules. Many technology industry analysts and corporate executives believe that the future of cloud computing will inevitably include new regulation. But what will the effects of that regulation be? On the one hand, regulation may consist of rules that will help the average consumer of cloud services by improving those services, ensuring auditability, and creating a business case for security. But as organizations consider how to best leverage computing on demand, regulation could drive up the cost for a cloud service provider to deliver, thus undermining the business cases for using cloud computing, such as pay-by-the-drink and no capital investment accounting.

The intent of regulation is to level the playing field. Compliance and security are difficult and expensive. This is precisely the reason that organizations will want to plan for what might be coming by applying best practices and standards ahead of potential mandates. Organizations should pay attention to the discussions about how best to control the behavior of vendors and consumers of cloud services. One must care about this and get involved with creating the standards and guidance to that end. Being a trustworthy organization is important because it is a market advantage. By thinking about what regulation is, why it occurs, and what standards the market may demand, a company or agency will best position itself for the future.

The community (consumers, vendors, and regulators) must consider existing regulation requirements, regulatory frameworks, best practices, and other legal and corporate obligations (in addition to possible new regulation). Such considerations will bring up the important questions unique to an organization, such as: *Does the categorization of an information system and the selection of security controls need to change based on the location of the computing power leveraged? If that location cannot be geographically pinpointed, how can controls be monitored?*

Answers to questions like these should help an organization to form a plan and expectations for the future.

WHAT IS REGULATION?

The concepts of regulation, framework, benchmark, and standards are not the same, but they are closely related.

A security benchmark (sometimes a standard) is the clarified baseline that can be used as a means of prescribing a specific setting or configuration that can mitigate specific risks. These standards are typically technical and put forth as a common best practice by a community.

There are a number of benchmarks, which are prescriptive sources of IT security settings for specific devices or applications (e.g., Windows Servers, UNIX Servers, Cisco Routers, and Oracle DBMS), such as:

- Center for Internet Security (CIS) benchmark guidance
- Defense Information Security Agency (DISA)—Checklists, Security Technical Information Guides (STIG)

- National Institute of Standards and Technology (NIST)—Federal Information Protection Standards (FIPS)
- National Security Agency (NSA)—Security Hardening Guidelines
- Vendors (various)—hardening/security best practices (e.g. Microsoft, Cisco, IBM, etc.)

Early adopters of security benchmarks are typically well situated to address framework and regulation developed afterward. Familiarity with benchmarks provides the business with an understanding of what controls work and what does not work in their environment. Since most auditors look to compliance with benchmarks as an indication of strong security settings, benchmark compliance benefits those businesses that can discuss them confidently.

A security framework is a more process- and topic-oriented guidance than a benchmark standard. A framework endeavors to describe a range of security areas to address security for the system. Unlike a benchmark, a framework may require administrative (process) or procedural controls in addition to technical controls. Many frameworks speak of *security objectives* rather than prescriptive actions.

Many security frameworks are enforced by industry or become the basis for law. These include:

- PCI—Payment Card Industry—for businesses who process credit cards
- NERC—National Electric Reliability Council—for utilities
- ISO/IEC 27001:2005—Information Security Management Systems Requirements—a framework for general IT systems security
- COBIT—Control Objectives for Information and related Technology—an IT Security and best practices framework

As with benchmarks, businesses that are early adopters of security frameworks have an easier time adapting to regulations. The business may be able to show compliance to a law and face easier audits by becoming certified as performing to the framework. In addition, frameworks often address the oversight functions of security governance, which is seen as a mature form of security and security management in the modern business.

A regulation is a rule or law. As a law, there is a consequence for not abiding, and the act of policing the law is called compliance. Often, a framework is referenced by a regulation (e.g., SOX → COSO/COBIT, UK CoCo → ISO27001). This is to provide both the user and the compliance auditor with guidelines that help orient good behavior and, hopefully, better security.

The intent of regulation is often broadly protective—for instance, to protect citizens, to protect shareholder value, to ensure corporate responsibility, and to create punishments and disincentive for wrongdoing and recklessness. In the United States, there exist a number of security regulations for business and governments including the following:

Federal Information Security Management Act

This 2002 legislation for IT security of U.S. government data at federal agencies was created to improve all aspects of system security for federal agencies of the United States. To some degree, it links security to funding, with the intent of raising overall protections and forcing greater oversight to wasteful and unsecure IT practices.

The Federal Information Security Act of 2002 (FISMA) requires compliance to federal guidance—typically, the *Special Publications* created by NIST. The security process defined is called *Certification and Accreditation* and includes a process to categorize data and systems for risk and apply appropriate controls, addressing development, operations, and shut down. The controls include all aspects of system security—17 *families* of controls from Access Control to Disaster Recovery—but do not address cloud computing directly.[1]

Sarbanes-Oxley Law

This 2002 legislation for secure reporting systems in publically traded firms was created to raise the reporting requirements on public companies and their accounting firms, with the intent to increase their accountability and transparency, and therefore strengthen public confidence in their performance.

The Sarbanes-Oxley Law (SOX) regulation requires assurance controls on data systems that are used to compute and report financial information. Meeting a SOX compliance requirement means abiding by compliance frameworks such as COSO or COBIT, and prescribe controls commiserate with risks to the reporting capability. This law does not address cloud computing.[2]

Health Information Privacy Accountability Act

This 1996 legislation for health-care security and privacy was created to ensure national standards for health-care transactions and records. Updated in the 2009 American Recovery and Reinvestment Act (ARRA/HITECH), the Health Information Privacy Accountability Act (HIPAA) rules now extend to additional businesses that support health-care.

HIPAA compliance requires a focus on safeguards for private, personal data captured or processed by the health-care industry. Compliance controls for data processing include the use of best practice systems hardening and can reflect prescription from sources such as CIS or DISA. HIPAA does not address cloud computing but has provisions for service providers that could include cloud vendors.

Graham/Leach/Bliley Act

This 1999 legislation for banking safeguards and privacy protections was created to enable consolidation in the financial services industry. It contains a number of provisions intended to protect the consumer information of the customers of these diversified institutions.

Graham/Leach/Bliley Act (GLBA) compliance is similar to HIPAA in that it focuses on controls that focus on maintaining control of privacy data and prescribes a risk assessment to apply appropriate controls on servers and data processing and storage of data. This law does not address cloud computing.

Privacy Laws

There are a number of privacy-specific laws that are found at state and federal levels, such as: Massachusetts 201 CMR 17.00, which prescribes specific data processing controls and behavior; and the Electronic Communications Privacy Act (ECPA), 1986 legislation which was created to restrict government access to private communications, with specific reference to e-mail. This law covers the collection of communications data and is often invoked during legal discovery process.

Not one of these regulations strictly addresses cloud technology, although they do speak to the use of third parties performing data processing, privacy and data protection, and the transfer of risk under the law. These are themes that will affect the use of international movement of data and services and in particular speak to the essence of cloud computing.

Countries have found that data and business do not always recognize national borders, so the regulatory and legal systems must be in harmony if they are to be effective. Harmonization is critical since cyber crime and criminal behavior often move to national borders where perpetrators have the most freedom to act and the least risk of being caught or prosecuted.

Some interesting international regulations include:

1. UK[3] and EU IT Security Compliance directives and privacy laws, such as:
    a. HMG Security Policy Framework (Oct 2009)—provides a U.S. NIST-similar framework to define risk/impact level of data and systems
    b. UK—The Privacy and Electronic Communications (EC Directive) Regulations 2003
    c. EU Data Protection Directive 95/46/EC (1995)—provides essential privacy and data processing law to protect citizen data from being abused
2. PCI[4]—new versions are authored triennially and are international in scope
3. JSOX—a Japanese[5] version of the SOX-type regulation, which maps to COSO-like objectives and similar audit considerations
4. Monetary Authority of Singapore[6]—publishing a host of guidelines and laws that affect a number of computer/IT and security issues, such as Electronic Transactions Act (Cap. 88), which controls:
    a. Electronic contracts
    b. Electronic records and signatures
    c. Secure electronic records and signatures
    d. Effect of digital signatures and duties relating to such signatures
    e. Duties of certification authorities and their subscribers
    f. Regulation of certification authorities
    g. Government use of electronic records and signatures
    h. Liability of network service providers

Since a move to cloud computing means that data is internationally portable and computations are powered by a computing grid that spans countries and continents, any single compliance effort undertaken might have to consider the impact of global regulation.

WHY DO REGULATIONS OCCUR?

Regulation is seen as a direct reaction to the failure of security programs. For example, SOX is often attributed to the accounting debacle at Enron. In that case, the authority (SEC) determined that the firm had not been able to police itself; a process prescribed had not been performed, resulting in harm to a community (in this case, shareholders). Because the problem was seen as systemic and wide spread, the resulting regulations were created to audit that the procedures would be executed, and broad controls would be installed. The Public Company Accounting Oversight Board (PCAOB), a non-profit organization, was formed to create specific rules or controls as well as a framework for publically-traded firms to follow and implement. And SOX auditors were trained to perform audits to meet the intent of the regulation.

PCAOB did not create a security framework in a vacuum; rather, they looked to the *best practice* framework (COSO) already in place. This allowed the PCAOB the ability to work quickly to set the guidelines and rules for audit; the use of existing best practices allowed for rapid adoption and buy-in. Ease of implementation is important when a security team is looking for widespread adoption of a framework across its business.

What was the result? The development of a SOX compliance program and supporting industry, as well as a sense that the industry is more secure, behavior is more consistent, and stakeholders are more certain of financial reporting. While it is not a perfect system, the result has been much greater security in several firms, and a compliance program with regulators who can specify the mechanics and intent of the rules.

It may be true that regulation often occurs when a community grows to a certain size and complexity. This is analogous to a driving speed limit. It is the people who do not abide by the rules who make life difficult and dangerous for everyone else. While obeying the speed limit rule does not make bad drivers good, or guarantee that the roads are safe, speed limit laws do provide a guideline, predictability, and ramifications for those who do not obey.

Some Key Takeaways

- Regulation arises when there is complexity and (perceived) high risk.
- Regulation needs frameworks and benchmark standards to provide guidance and compliance programs.

THE REAL WORLD—A MIXING BOWL

It is common for businesses to use prescriptive sources (starting with security benchmark standards) to harden their systems or build their own custom standards for their IT systems, and to marry these to the requirements found in regulation appropriate to their business. For instance, a business that must comply with SOX and PCI will wisely try to meet these compliance requirements with a single effort rather than undergo two separate attempts to meet the compliance reporting requirements of each program.

Furthermore, business is broadly encouraged by regulations, frameworks, and best practices to execute a risk assessment to adjust specific controls and to determine which controls are most important to the security of the system(s) overall. A risk assessment procedure does not take the place of prescribed controls; rather, it informs the organization of the controls required and can help prioritize and adjust controls to provide appropriate and compliant systems.

It is important that controls and risk assessment be addressed by any future regulation of the cloud. If a cloud vendor cannot provide controls required by compliance and regulation or risk assessment, then it will encounter highly dissatisfied customers, or possibly legal liability and fewer customers.

Likewise, future regulation can provide global standards in compliance that will help both clients and providers to address the increasing audit demands by customers who try to enforce their specific needs, and by vendors who have little motivation to abide by laws of another country. New suggestions, as seen in the recent ENISA (European National Information Security Agency) articles[7] address potential global cloud regulation issues, such as:

- Mismatched data protection laws and directives
- Customer breach notification law and penalty after an incident
- Liability exemptions for intermediaries (cloud providers) in the business models arising from e-commerce
- How to support the creation of minimum data protection standards and privacy certification schemes in an international setting

Waiting for regulation to solve the problems may be appropriate for some businesses, but businesses already engaged in cloud computing should endeavor to bridge the problems. This involves early adoption of security standards and frameworks that work for their business. It involves research and work with their cloud providers for common controls and national regulation issues (especially privacy) that must be met by third parties regardless of location. What makes a business secure is not merely the appropriate adherence to regulations, frameworks, and benchmarks. Security must work for the organization's specific risks and also be supported by development of a harmonized international framework security program to address the creation of standards, the application of risk assessments and a security framework, and the reporting for applicable regulation that can mitigate security risk. In the business world today the security program is likely to be on the front line—either to defend the organization from cyber threats, address the lawsuit to prove behavior of systems, or show that IT controls are in place to meet the regulatory requirements. The security program is the critical component and must be able to work and be part of the strategy of the organization as a whole to meet the ever-increasing security demands of doing secure business today.

Some Key Takeaways

- The cloud vendors must recognize that clients have to meet the requirements of existing compliance programs, which do not reflect the technology or capabilities of the cloud.
- The businesses that have to meet the requirements of one or more compliance programs should be very cautious to use cloud technologies to assure that they meet the security requirements prescribed by the matrix of compliance requirements found in frameworks and benchmark standards.

 THE REGULATION STORY

The cloud computing industry must deal with existing regulation (such as SOX, PCI, etc.) as part of addressing client requirements. But the cloud computing phenomenon itself is likely to cause new regulation.

As with any computing investment, consideration of the financial return is a primary driver. In the case of the cloud, vendors have developed a number of new and innovative business models to make software, hardware, or operational functions outsourced for the client. The list of promises from cloud models is impressive. The list includes cost savings on equipment, setup, administration, licensing, and much more. So, it is particularly important that the pains associated with cloud solutions be fairly minimal.

The story of many regulatory programs is a gradual one. First, the market sets standard benchmarks that stabilize, followed by frameworks, and then regulation. The standards phase typically initiates when the industry (vendors, manufacturers) provides common methods to address problem areas. This can be seen in new product lines, such as VMware's release of recommended security standards for their virtualization tools.[8] As clients start using these standards, they will test the value of these standards to meet security requirements.

The next step is the development of frameworks, which might be developed in conjunction with specific standards to develop best practices for business.

These frameworks can be seen, for example, in development of the PCI framework used to assure that companies processing or handling credit card data protect it throughout the business and not just at a specific device or component. Frameworks closely resemble regulation because they often are associated with the audit process or verification steps that would be used to comply with that framework. Sometimes, frameworks are directly referenced by regulation.

The final phase, regulation, is often preceded by a sense of increasing frustration: a sense that frameworks are sufficient, but that full compliance of the industry is needed to protect the public good or level the playing field for those who will not abide by best practices.[9] It is not uncommon that a single significant incident precedes a regulatory development, such as the Enron financial meltdown, or the significant breach of privacy information that has been linked to GLBA and HIPAA regulation.

For cloud computing, consumers of the offerings should start looking for evidence of standards and frameworks. This evidence of emergence can be found when looking at the Cloud Security Alliance (CSA), for instance. CSA has done some research in order to compile a list, which they call the *Biggest Threats to the Cloud:*[10]

Threat #1: Abuse and Nefarious Use of Cloud Computing
Threat #2: Insecure Interfaces and APIs
Threat #3: Malicious Insiders
Threat #4: Shared Technology Issues
Threat #5: Data Loss or Leakage
Threat #6: Account or Service Hijacking
Threat #7: Unknown Risk Profile

The list has the strong basics for the development of a standards and a possible security framework for cloud computing. The question many in the industry and clients should consider is, "do *these risks constitute reason for regulation?*"

If they do, then perhaps it is wise to consider the work of a standards organization such as the NIST. This organization is very experienced in the regulation story: providing the initial research on a wide variety of technologies, and developing or assisting in the development of standards and frameworks that support the regulation of industry. Many governmental regulatory bodies, including a number of international government regulatory bodies, reference the work done by NIST to justify and support the development of regulation.

NIST has conducted a number of significant studies of cloud computing that support the conclusions of the CSA. The essence of recent presentations and work by the cloud computing working groups[11] is that cloud development must focus on trust, multitenancy, encryption, compliance to solve security and privacy concerns in using third-party clouds with sensitive data, and problems of security boundaries and security compliance (e.g., HIPAA, FISMA, SOX).

In particular, NIST brings up the broad scope of issues—technical, managerial, and international—that must be addressed in cloud computing. The list seems endless, but the first items on most lists do seem intractable by merely applying standards or common frameworks. These are the concerns that have to address privacy and international compliance. NIST stipulates that first stage for developing security for the cloud will have to address:

- Data dispersal and international privacy laws
- EU Data Protection Directive and U.S. Safe Harbor program
- Exposure of data to foreign government and data subpoenas
- Data retention issues

Privacy

Privacy really has become a significant international business issue—and not only for the cloud. Privacy concepts are not universally agreed upon, and between the United States and Europe, there are essential and significant barriers to trade based on this issue. At their cores, the United States' position and the European Union's (EU) differ in basic privacy tenants associated by a right to privacy (as seen in default opt-in in U.S., opt-out in EU). For instance, the United States is seen as having a hostile stance towards privacy, as evidenced by U.S. government programs that can monitor the communications of American citizens. On the other end of the spectrum are business rules in Europe that protect the identity of employees of international businesses even from their parent (non-EU) office.

Since these privacy laws differ between countries, there have been some EU-U.S. *safe harbor* programs set up to allow international firms to work between countries through privacy-specific contracts, but these are not seen as being highly effective. The problems are that trust between countries on the issue of privacy is low, and it will likely be necessary to harmonize laws between governments to support the use of data subpoenas, monitoring, and international terrorism efforts.

This sparks an issue for the cloud computing business model that cannot be solved by standards and frameworks alone. Since a number of cloud models can call for storage of data and applications that cross national borders, it will be imperative that the privacy laws are addressed in legal manners that can be reliably defined and enforced. And it will likely have to be left to international regulation to do this.

International Export Law and Interoperable Compliance

A tenet of security conformance is the ability to audit and validate compliance to contract, standard, framework, or law. If this mechanism does not exist, few will risk the venture of releasing corporate, client, or transactions information into the cloud for potential loss or abuse. And *blind* use of cloud computing is more risky than ever, given the rise of interconnected cloud systems.

For instance, users of a cloud solution could export controlled technical data without proper government authorization every time they save a document—if the server or service being used to store or process the data is outside the United States and in a location where an export license would be required to export the technology. The resulting penalties can be significant—civil fines range from $250,000 to $1 million depending on the type of information—and criminal penalties can be set for controlled data exported without license.[12] Both clients and vendors need to consider the risks of inadvertent export control violation, since it does not matter if the intent was to violate export controls.[13] And since much of the commercial software in the United States is under export control, this risk potential is enormous.

To this end, some cloud vendors have endeavored to meet a specific auditable stance (e.g., PCI,[14] FISMA, SOX), which brings up two important issues:

1. If a service provider can accommodate a compliance mandate for one customer, can the accommodation(s) be used for other customers? (And how can this be instantiated reliably?)
2. What about the use of multiple cloud providers (working in an interoperable fashion) in achieving and maintaining compliance to a standard or export law?

These questions underscore that the export problem cannot be solved easily by the vendors alone. The need for compliance programs to address complex cloud computing scenarios and to define the compliance requirements with regard to that new business model is important to the success of the cloud industry as a whole.

The need for a regulation that reflects the demands of a flexible business model has been addressed by some vendors through use of the SAS 70 or SSAE 16 (Type II) audit, which looks to the specific environment of the vendor to determine the auditor's requirement.[15] This creates a challenge, as it forces the auditor to ascertain whether process is consistent between vendors. It is difficult for auditors, who must be able to address a complexity of technologies and requirements and interconnected cloud environments. Such a lack of consistency is likely to cause greater frustration in the industry overall and is thus likely to meet the criteria for national and international regulation in the future.

EFFECTIVE AUDIT

Audit is an important function in a modern, governance-based organization. If audits are conducted without mind to business models, they are just punitive. An abundance of auditing conducted for the sake of finding errors has led the general public to think of financial audits with fear and anxiety. It has come to be perceived as all stick and no carrot. But this is an unfortunate point of view, and there is an increased recognition across many businesses that governance and compliance are part of a modern business model and should not be feared. Rather, audit can and should be a function to validate controls of real and important risks. An auditor can teach an organization how to conduct business effectively and safely if he is engaged as a part of the strategy team. In this governance-driven model, an auditor takes the approach that risk management and organizational self-examination is the purpose of his work. Audit can be seen as part of the solution to staying secure, attracting customers, and remaining compliant to regulation.

The real question about audit is how to use the mechanism effectively. One way to do this is to involve the audit management and planning function into the cloud computing plans from the onset. This role would focus on risk assessment of functions that might be applied to cloud services, to address mitigating controls early in the service definition.

The risk assessment of applications sent to the cloud also can bring up alternative strategies for cloud services—such as putting non-critical systems or data onto the cloud for testing and monitoring for control mechanisms. This can also be used as a lower cost model for approaching cloud services.

Certainly the audit involvement (such as internal audit) can be critical for the design of systems and services in the cloud that will meet regulations, which require or prescribe specific safeguards that did not take cloud into consideration when written. The rise of privacy laws across the globe and the effect of international differences in legal recourse are affecting the ability to use cloud services.

Auditors also can bring value by examining a worst-case scenario: bringing experience and methods to help test the cloud vendor mechanisms to address incidents, to test service level agreements (SLAs), and to address other legal events. It is the audit function that may be able to determine before an event that specific controls are ineffective, inappropriate, or costly for a vendor or client.

 ## IDENTIFYING RISK

Mentioned throughout this chapter are the concepts of risk identification and mitigation. Regulation, standards, and frameworks do not eliminate risk for the vendor or client of cloud computing. In fact, as pointed out, current regulation does little to address cloud specific risks and it will take time for future standards, frameworks, and regulation to help.

To assist those new to the process of identifying risk, Exhibit 8.1 may serve as a starting point for those addressing cloud-specific considerations and possible mitigations.

 ## IN SUMMARY

Cloud computing remains a little like the Wild West for both the client and the vendor. There are few rules, lots of potential, and a growing desire within many to take advantage of a new business model. Since this landscape is similar to other industries, consumers of cloud computing can predict the need to address both the requirements of current laws and the potential for the creation of new regulation of this industry.

The reason why regulation may be necessary in the cloud computing industry is the need to provide a fair playing field for all players, as well as to address certain problems that can arise when attempting to harmonize regulation across national borders.

EXHIBIT 8.1 Cloud Risks and Mitigations

Risk	Description	Mitigation strategy
Data Protection	This includes protection of availability, confidentiality, and integrity.	Cloud services must provide strong controls such as logging, backup and recovery, and encryption to assure data protection
Compliance with Regulation, Framework, or Standard	If cloud services are to be used for data or services covered by regulation.	Cloud services must provide assurances that they can meet regulatory requirements and be audited by client or third party for verification of controls.
Loss of Control	By definition, the client loses control of resources, so address this appropriately.	SLA and contractual agreements should address how the vendor and client will address issues of administration, incident handling, verification of data protection, and resource availability.
Flexible Data and Services Model	Adjusting in early days of using cloud services is a norm.	In a worst-case scenario, movement of data and services may require roll-back on a cloud contract— either to another vendor or to bring back in house. Plan for this in order to avoid massive risk and costs.

It is certain that standards will arise in the field of cloud computing as vendors and other key players come to agreement on ways to address security and compliance problems. Certain existing domain regulations—such as PCI, SOX, EU Privacy Directive, and U.S. Export laws—will likely amend or clarify their rules to help provide guidance in using cloud resources. Corporations and agencies alike should pay close attention to the development of standards as a way to lessen the burdens of eventual regulation.

Key players in the industry, such as the CSA, ENISA, ISACA, and NIST, are likely to help clarify risk, best practices, and standards in regard to cloud computing. Staying abreast of these sources and engaged with them, in addition to any regulatory authorities with whom an organization already works, is strongly advised.

As with any security requirement and focus, an organization should create a risk assessment and security framework that accounts for data portability, shared and distributed computational capability, and billing practices based on usage and outcomes rather than physical presence. With such guidelines and protections in place, the agency or corporation will be best positioned to assess and address the impacts of global regulation.

Because there are so few standards defined today, there are few regulations. This presents an opportunity for influence and leadership that could propel an organization to a trustworthy position with market leaders, industry leaders, and customers.

 NOTES

1. NIST is working on a cloud computing Special Publication, which may assist in developing a framework for using control families in a cloud environment. See recent material at http://csrc.nist.gov/groups/SNS/cloud-computing/.
2. ISACA (author of COBIT IT Framework) is starting to address cloud security and auditing.
3. UK Data Protection Act 1998, www.legislation.gov.uk/ukpga/1998/29/contents, and The Privacy and Electronic Communications (EC Directive) Regulations 2003, www.legislation.gov.uk/uksi/2003/2426/contents/made. Find the Cabinet Office Security Framework at www.eurim.org.uk/activities/ig/idg/SecurityPolicyFramework.pdf.
4. www.pcisecuritystandards.org/.
5. www.meti.go.jp/english/policy/index.html.
6. www.ida.gov.sg/Policies%20and%20Regulation/20060416174257.aspx.
7. See the ENISA report, Cloud Computing: Benefits, Risks and Recommendations for Information Security (May 2010).
8. For vSphere v4, http://blogs.vmware.com/security/2010/04/vsphere-40-hardening-guide-released.html.
9. www.computerworld.com/s/article/9175102/Frustrations_with_cloud_computing_mount.
10. CSA Threat Analysis, www.cloudsecurityalliance.org/topthreats/csathreats.v1.0.pdf.

11. See NIST presentations, http://csrc.nist.gov/groups/SNS/cloud-computing/; and the NIST Cloud Computing Working groups Wiki site, http://collaborate.nist.gov/twiki-cloud-computing/bin/view/CloudComputing/WebHome.

12. http://hosted-voip.tmcnet.com/feature/articles/72410-exporting-into-clouds-export-compliance-issues-associated-with.htm.

13. According to the Export Administrative Regulations 15 C.F.R. § 734.2(b)(1), and the International Trafficking in Arms Regulations ("ITAR"), 22 C.F.R. § 120.17(a)(1).

14. Rackspace PCI compliance made a splash, but it doesn't mean a free ride for PCI clients, www.rackspacecloud.com/blog/2009/03/05/cloud-hosting-is-secure-for-take-off-mosso-enables-the-spreadsheet-store-an-online-merchant-to-become-pci-compliant/

15. See Google passes its initial SAS Type II, http://googleenterprise.blogspot.com/2008/11/sas-70-type-ii-for-google-apps.html. Google has since achieved FISMA compliance for part of its offering to federal clients.

REFERENCES

ENISA web site: www.enisa.europa.eu/ (accessed March 19, 2011).

Cloud Computing Risk Assessment (2009), www.enisa.europa.eu/act/rm/files/deliverables/cloud-computing-risk-assessment (accessed March 19, 2011).

Cloud Security Alliance (CSA) web site, http://cloudsecurityalliance.org/ (accessed March 19, 2011).

CSA: Security Guidance for Critical Areas of Focus in Cloud Computing V2.1 (December 2009), https://cloudsecurityalliance.org/csaguide.pdf (accessed March 19, 2011).

CSA Cloud Security Alliance GRC Stack is a link site to CSA tools for audit/compliance and governance, https://cloudsecurityalliance.org/Research.html (accessed March 19, 2011).

U.S. National Institute of Standards and Technology (NIST) web site on Cloud Computing, including cloud definitions, links to forums and other cloud security information. http://csrc.nist.gov/groups/SNS/cloud-computing/ (accessed March 19, 2011).

NIST Recommended Security Controls—FISMA (2009), http://csrc.nist.gov/publications/nistpubs/800-53-Rev3/sp800-53-rev3-final.pdf (accessed March 19, 2011).

NIST Cloud Computing Working Group(s) have forum and information, http://collaborate.nist.gov/twiki-cloud-computing/bin/view/CloudComputing/WebHome (accessed March 19, 2011).

Public Company Accounting Oversight Board (PCAOB) web site on compliance with SOX and addressing current issues, http://pcaobus.org/Pages/default .aspx (accessed March 19, 2011).

ISACA site for information on the COBIT Framework, www.isaca.org/Knowledge-Center/COBIT/Pages/Overview.aspx (accessed March 19, 2011).

Singapore Government IDA, www.ida.gov.sg/Policies%20and%20Regulation/20060416174257.aspx (accessed March 19, 2011).

UK Government guidance on Code of Compliance, www.publicservice.co.uk/propdf/Credant%20PRO.pdf (accessed March 19, 2011). Also, UK Data Protection Act 1998: www.legislation.gov.uk/ukpga/1998/29/contents, and The Privacy and Electronic Communications (EC Directive) Regulations 2003 at www.legislation.gov.uk/uksi/2003/2426/contents/made. Find the Cabinet Office Security Framework at www.eurim.org.uk/activities/ig/idg/Security
PolicyFramework.pdf.

PCI Security Standards Council regulates credit card data—web site provides guidance and information. www.pcisecuritystandards.org/ (accessed March 19, 2011).

Protiviti report on Japanese Government regulation known as J-SOX http://protiviti.com/ja-JP/Downloads/flashreport/JSOX_FlashReport_02E.pdf (accessed March 19, 2011).

VMWare posts compliance and security hardening guidance blog, http://blogs.vmware.com/security/2010/04/vsphere-40-hardening-guide-released.html (accessed March 19, 2011).

"Cloud Computing: An Auditor's Perspective" (2009) by Sailesh Gadia, CISA, ACA, CPA, *CIPP ISACA Journal* 6.

"Do Federal Security Regulations Help?" (2006) by Bruce Schneier, www.schneier.com/essay-141.html (accessed March 19, 2011).

"Frustrations with Cloud Computing Mount" (2010) by Patrick Thibodeau www.computerworld.com/s/article/9175102/Frustrations_with_cloud_computing_mount (accessed March 19, 2011).

"SAS70 Type II for Google Apps" (2008) by Eran Feigenbaum http://googleenterprise.blogspot.com/2008/11/sas-70-type-ii-for-google-apps.html (accessed March 19, 2011).

"Exporting into the Clouds: Export Compliance Issues Associated with Cloud Computing" (2010) by Eric R. McClafferty, http://hosted-voip.tmcnet.com/feature/articles/72410-exporting-into-clouds-export-compliance-issues-associated-with.htm (accessed March 19, 2011).

"Cloud Hosting Is Secure for Take-off: Mosso Enables The Spreadsheet Store, an Online Merchant, to become PCI Compliant" (2009) by Angela Bartels, www.rackspacecloud.com/blog/2009/03/05/cloud-hosting-is-secure-for-take-off-mosso-enables-the-spreadsheet-store-an-online-merchant-to-become-pci-compliant/ (accessed March 19, 2011).

CHAPTER NINE

Cloud Morphing

Shaping the Future of Cloud Computing Security and Audit

Liam Lynch
Tammi Hayes

TWO TYPICAL QUESTIONS about clouds are: what's new about this? and isn't this just another word for outsourcing?

The quick answer is yes and no.

During a red team exercise in 2008, in which an independent team assessed the security of an organization to provide a realistic view of security readiness, a discussion of impending cloud computing use got the attention of a few security professionals. Over the ensuing two-year period, many types of cloud plans have come and gone, but the need for securing the cloud gained traction in the security industry resulting in the formation of the Cloud Security Alliance (CSA).

The group has done a lot of work to document where security professionals need to concentrate their work in securing the cloud. Several of the domains that have been worked on directly or indirectly affect an organization's ability to audit technology platforms while they reside in the cloud.

In this chapter, the *cloud* refers to an outsourced platform component for any business or personal need. To that end, there have been many statements over the last year about why this is different from other outsourced models that have been around for decades. The answer is fairly simple; in the past, businesses and individuals have outsourced a discrete technology component such as customer relationship management or financial journaling. The new cloud considerations and needs lean toward outsourcing anything and everything. Auditing, for example, has added complexity for outsourced business platforms. In the case of outsourced financial journaling and processing, a Sarbanes-Oxley (SOX) audit has to follow the path of financial information integrity to a third party. The architecture of SOX compliance is increasingly challenging as more business processes, including those that are regulated, go into the cloud.

This chapter also discusses morphology as it relates to cloud computing and business processes. Morphing something is analogous to morphing in geographic map technology and programming languages. The idea is that you have something such as a structure and processes or data, and by applying a different process or changing the declaration of the structure, process, or data, you alter the behavior or the visual characteristics—but you still have the same structure, process, or data. Cloud computing vendors have to morph and business processes also have to morph to ensure the security of data and applications, as well as the ability to effectively run compliance: in other words, audit what the business has in the cloud.

 WHERE IS THE DATA?

Data in the cloud must have its own eyes and a Global Positioning System (GPS). Data must be able to determine who is looking at it or changing it as well as know where in the world it is being stored. We are at a point in technology where there will be a fundamental change is the standards and technology in data processing.

Prior to cloud computing, data resided in database management systems that were under the control of the organization that was responsible for the data. The data generally sits at rest in the database and the management system can audit who interacts with the data at the time the interaction occurs. With regard to the database, the management system, the computers, and the networks, the processing runs within physical locations owned by the organization. In the cloud, this is no longer the case.

An audit of the data processing systems of a regulated set of data can produce reports and demonstrate easily if a data processing system complies with a standard or a regulatory set of requirements. Everything from physical security of buildings, to access control policies in software, to the authorization controls of infrastructure and database management systems, is directly and easily viewed and demonstrated. In the cloud, however, a different organization has control over all components.

Take, for example, an audit need to demonstrate that only employees of your company can enter a data center and only employees with a need to enter the data center can do so. A cloud vendor with thousands or hundreds of thousands of customers can't physically make it possible for site visits by each of their customers and their auditors. The vendor also has control over the database management systems, computers, and networks that your applications use. So why would anyone want to do this?

The CSA founders asked the same question and determined that security had to enable cloud computing use. The reasons that any company would use the cloud are based primarily on finances.

The cloud enables cheap agile innovation. The concept is called *fail fast*. Before the cloud, a company or entrepreneur needed large capital investment to create a new product or service on the Internet. A new company needed large capital investment just to start the company with servers, computers, e-mail systems, and collaboration tools. With the cloud, an entrepreneur can self-fund an idea and demonstrate it live in a very short period of time. A company with a new idea can realize the same benefit by not having to invest money in more servers, networks, and potentially, data centers or new data center space.

There is also the cost savings of existing technology that a company can use to increase profit and reinvest back into their business. A higher margin due to lower IT costs is a significant driver for moving to the cloud.

An entrepreneur can also get very good data for their market research section of their business plan by having a new product running instead of simply having documentation about the product. A new product can be quickly built and placed into a public cloud inexpensively without having to own infrastructure.

Anyone can put a new product into a public cloud quickly and determine if it has any value. If the idea looks like it won't work early on, then there haven't been large sums of money used, leading to a fail-fast agile development.

A SHIFT IN THINKING

The benefits to using cloud technology aren't always specifically visible. Virtualization technology has been allowing companies to reduce the number of computers they have to manage by allowing computers to run many *virtual* servers. Cloud-enabling technologies, like virtualization, allow cost savings by outsourcing, but the same technologies also allow for cost savings in *owned* systems.

Now, let's examine some of the challenges. The CSA has spent a great deal of effort on documenting cloud security challenges by organizing them into domains. With two iterations of documenting the challenges, performing research, and seeding two separate efforts, the CSA and its members have done an excellent job to help professionals focus on cloud security.

One project that was spun off in 2010 is the CloudAudit initiative, which is meant to provide guidance and standards for audit requirements for cloud providers, so that the cloud vendor has the means to demonstrate how audit requirements are being met. Cloud computing represents the broad shift toward computing operating as a utility. Just as the electrical industry went through a revolution a century ago, which created a distinction and segregation between power production and power transmission, cloud computing today means that cloud providers, both large and small, are delivering computing services to consumers that can be ordered and provisioned on demand. While the metered service, elasticity of demand, and multitenancy has many aspects of a traditional utility, the complexity of cloud computing far exceeds these models and requires much new thinking to appropriately secure it.

Cloud computing initially rose not as a new technology, but rather as an economic and business model. Moore's Law has continued to drive down the costs of computing and drive up its price performance. This has meant that while any business could afford to purchase significant computing capacity, the problem that Moore's Law has not solved is the cost of ownership of computing. At the same time, large-scale Internet-based services have made great progress in developing an economy of scale in managing many millions of users, applications, and computers. Companies such as Amazon.com looked for business opportunities to capitalize on their efficiencies and sell excess computing capacity. To complement this trend, the bandwidth investments of the 1990s and the rise of Service Oriented Architecture (SOA) have created the connectivity and application foundation to feasibly deliver computing capabilities from third-party service providers in a flexible manner.

The major security significance of computing as a utility is that we are separating the organizations with legal responsibility for digital information from third-party organizations, that are the actual, physical custodians of that information. This reality disrupts what we think we know about information security best practices, and forces the practitioner to rethink what is necessary to secure critical assets and systems in a cloud environment—from very broad governance principles to very granular security controls.

Cloud Security Alliance

The CSA is a non-profit organization with a global presence that was formed to create the necessary ecosystem to assure a secure and trusted cloud. CSA is focused upon research, education, best practices, and certification to make this vision a reality. Among the key deliverables from CSA are the following:

- *CSA Security Guidance for Critical Areas of Focus in Cloud Computing.* This whitepaper is a broad catalogue of cloud security issues and best practices. It has been translated into several languages and serves as the foundation for CSA's other research initiatives.
- *CSA Controls Matrix.* This working group is chartered with maintaining the definitive list of security controls applicable to cloud computing, both from a customer and provider perspective. The controls matrix output is delivered in machine-readable format to facilitate integrate with commercial off-the-shelf and homegrown security tools.
- *CSA Consensus Assessments Initiative.* This working group has released an assessments questionnaire that captures the key questions that must be asked of cloud providers to identify control areas and other important information a cloud customer must know. The questionnaire is derived from the CSA Guidance and Controls Matrix and is intended to simplify usage of these documents in real-world environments.
- *CSA Trusted Cloud Initiative.* This research project is creating reference models and provider certification criteria for secure and interoperable identity in the cloud. The root of many security issues within cloud computing relate back to building trust in the various logical and physical components. In many ways, the trust issue is addressed by providing an identity infrastructure that is provably secure and puts the control in the hands of the users, and yet is extended beyond the users into devices, applications, and data. The TCI reference model includes important concepts such as strong authentication, identity federation, and claims-based identity

management, but is also defining how identity should be integrated into other critical parts of the cloud systems, such as encryption. TCI also includes a broad set of principles relating to how identities should be governed, how identity providers should be accorded fair access to third-party cloud applications and several other areas.

- *CSA Chapters.* Chapter organizations are forming around the world to apply the key knowledge and best practices to regional and jurisdictional issues, using the native languages and leveraging the existing information technology communities.
- *Certificate of Cloud Security Knowledge (CCSK).* The CCSK is the first user certification, testing individual knowledge of important cloud security issues and solutions.

CloudAudit 1.0

A related and important initiative is CloudAudit. CloudAudit is an initiative to create a simple standard and application program interface (API) set to help operationalize much of the key practices, such as those articulated by the CSA, to help break through the transparency problem and create an achievable assurance of cloud providers. CloudAudit enables a provider to make assertions about a broad variety of security controls, and it does so in a way that allows both cloud customers and independent auditors to independently gather important information used for audits and risk assessments. The CloudAudit API allows this data gathering process to be automated, which is analogous to how network management consoles gather system health information through Simple Network Management Protocol (SNMP). This solves the scalability problem of cloud provider audit responses and allows the provider to protect proprietary intellectual property, while allowing customers to obtain real-time answers to assurance questions. As cloud providers instrument their offerings with CloudAudit, the entire industry can understand their security practices in a transparent manner. CloudAudit 1.0 has incorporated the CSA Controls Matrix into its name space definitions.

CLOUD MORPHING STRATEGIES

Security strategists have been working on developing ways to ensure security in the cloud, but also on ways in which audits can be done easily and efficiently.

As discussed earlier in this chapter, there are new components with which a cloud customer will need to become familiar. For customers of cloud platforms or users of virtualization technology, there are two new components that need security service as well as audit programs: the hypervisor and virtual machines.

Virtual Security

A hypervisor is a new software component that adds services to the base operating system on computers in a cloud environment. The hypervisor is responsible for providing services to one or more virtual machines. Virtual machines use the hypervisor to attach to system devices such as network and disk/storage area networks, as well as for CPU and memory. Before clouds, one operating system provided all these services. In cloud computing, the operating system now gets all its compute resources from a virtual machine, which in turn gets computing resources from a hypervisor.

An issue for security auditors is that virtual machines lead to either a public cloud or your own virtual environment. This is called multitenancy. Before the cloud, one computer ran one operating system and most likely one application. The computer would be grouped with other computers running the same application, and if required, segmented by a firewall. An auditor could review a firewall configuration and determine whether sufficient protection existed for an application.

In a multitenant environment, one computer can run a variety of operating systems—each on a virtual machine and each running a different application. Multitenancy is what creates the cost savings because in a cloud, more than one application for more than one purpose can exist on one physical computer (as opposed to one application per computer).

The issue is how to segment each running application from another adjacent application and how to secure a hypervisor and virtual machine? There are vendors working with virtualization companies to create virtual versions of security components such as firewalls and intrusion management, for example. One key differentiator for these virtual versions of security is how they can be virtually managed. Before the cloud, intrusion management and firewall products ran on their own hardware. In the cloud, they need to be dynamically assigned to hypervisors and virtual machines at a moment's notice.

The reason for dynamic assignment is the agile nature of cloud technology. If a business user can dynamically grow their product across a virtual environment in minutes, the security product has to be as available as the application it protects. Firewalls and intrusion management, in this example, need to be dynamically deployed when the application is deployed.

Applications are also protected by anti-malware scanning as well as by other security products, and they, too, need to be as dynamically deployable as the application. Morphing those products in addition to firewalls and intrusion products also needs to occur—if for no other reason than licensing. The cloud allows an application to grow in scale in a matter of minutes. CPU-based licensing doesn't work well when an environment grows from one CPU to a million in minutes.

Multitenant environments also have a reporting problem. Before the cloud, applications ran on servers and issues could be alarmed easily. Collection of issue data was easily assigned to an application running on a server. In the cloud, each computer can run many applications on a variety of operating systems. Events and messaging of issues has to be more granular than in the past, which leads to morphing of incident response, availability measurement, and many other programs. Programs need to change within an information security organization as well as within auditing organizations and their practices.

DATA IN THE CLOUD

Data in the cloud is what causes the most anxiety for a security professional. A privacy expert made a good point when discussing the cloud recently: "The best way to avoid a breach is to not store the information in the first place." This is certainly true, but a vast majority of Internet-based applications simply cannot run without storing data—data that is sensitive and personal.

Data in the cloud being stored certainly needs to be encrypted and the cryptographic keys should not be stored in the cloud. Data in the cloud needs to understand or at least deal with the geographic locale of the user providing the data. Global privacy regulations require that. The personal nature of data and all privacy regulations lead to a concrete conclusion about protecting stored data anywhere; there is a need to directly map identity to the management of data no matter where it is stored.

Who has access to data is an age-old problem, which is exacerbated by the cloud. A business that collects information needs to monitor the use of the data for legal reasons. A business that has employees with access to the data can monitor access and block and report on access violations. In the cloud, the business doesn't control the administrative employee and that complicates the audit process and also disables much of what a business would use to monitor and block access violations.

Data needs to be more active in its own existence and management. The data needs eyes and a GPS. Data processing will also have to go through a major innovation cycle before large-scale data is placed in the cloud. This is not just for information security but for the effectiveness of the global audit and regulatory compliance processes, as well.

In the cloud, identity and access management has become paramount. Data needs to be protected and information security needs to work with auditors and internal compliance initiatives to support audit programs.

Data is largely at rest. In applications, a small subset of personal data is actually used at any time. This fact indicates that most data of a personal or regulatory manner is a sitting duck. Database management systems simply let data at rest fall asleep. Data that is asleep is the data most at risk, and consequently, this is the data that is almost always breached.

CLOUD STORAGE

Cloud storage is currently modeled like a conventional relational database, or as loosely defined elements that can't be related other than how the customer needs the data related. Operations on the data have to be either moved into the cloud with the data or the data must move back and forth between the cloud and the user's premises for processing. If the data needs to be encrypted or secure in other ways, the customer must define how the protection scheme works and implement the security. Cloud storage, therefore, is limited in its usability and will cause much engineering in order to be used safely.

What if there were a way to use cloud storage that would allow the owner of any type of data to more easily integrate that data into existing processes, thereby providing security, auditability, and other forms of protection and control? There would need to be a way to model and structure the data, and runtime access would need to be enabled using existing data access technology.

A problem with database management systems has been centered on scalar attributes. In relational database management systems, scalar attribution has been the way to achieve scalability. In object to relational mapping, one common complaint has been the mapping of scalar types. A scalar type is a data element that is of a known quantity and length, such as an integer, a floating-point value, or a string. Large objects are not generally recognized as scalar attributes because their type is not known or their length is not known when the table is being designed. Using object-oriented methods, for example, within an instance of a class, the object can know the type (PDF, Word document, spreadsheet, etc.) and its length. This is because there's a method in the object that understands the large object, and the method is contained within the object. Objects can then represent anything tied to a method to make it scalar. With today's technology, especially in the cloud, we can make large scalar quantities look like older database scalar quantities.

In conventional database management systems, a large object that varies in what it contains has been called a blob or a clob. A *blob* is a binary large object and would be used to store data that is formatted in non-readable formats. A *clob* is a character large object and would be used to store data that is in text format, but just in large amounts up to a limit. The limit for a clob is larger than a database string type and could be in the gigabyte range.

Cloud storage will always need an underlying mechanism to contain raw data items in a way that the provider can support. What is also needed, however, is a way to morph a proprietary raw storage format and create a different way to control the data to allow better security and a way to audit who and what has access to the data.

Object databases maintain the ideas of data and operation encapsulation but object databases do not have ways to describe how security and audit can be achieved for the cloud. The cloud database adopts object-oriented techniques and extends those techniques for cloud deployment. By extending object database principles, to promote security and audit in the cloud, users and organizations can maintain their needs and compliance programs.

An object database infrastructure could be used in a widely distributed and secure way. Each object or collection of objects being stored has everything the object needs to maintain itself. Security, lifecycle, integrity, and collaboration are all contained within each object instance based upon a design criterion for storage needs. In this way, data could be distributed across a vast network and each object could collaborate with other objects across the network to maintain consistency. In the past, widely distributed networks were difficult but some uses of the idea could be used to evaluate performance and security using the object system. Today, with the cloud, this object system can be used for secure cloud storage.

To achieve a cloud-based data store, the schema uses object-oriented classes and models data elements as attributes. Since most current cloud storage mechanisms look like older relational blobs, and because it now makes sense to use an object database, any type of data can be put into the cloud and modeled using object-oriented techniques. The underlying storage mechanism of cloud data storage now maps nicely to object-orientation storage needs.

Database Classes in the Cloud

In order to introduce flexibility at the data level and enable systemic capabilities such as security, disaster recovery, and audit, an attribute is designed to encapsulate all the needs when a data element is described for storage. An attribute has a value and a type but also has policy capabilities for lifecycle management, cryptography, data consistency, disaster recovery, audit trail, and a process to determine the data's geographical location. An attribute in the new cloud database contains one too many attributes in a class where each attribute contains all data and operations needed to allow the data to exist in a cloud environment.

Classes in the cloud database encapsulate attributes and can control the policies and actions for values in the class at a high level (for all instances of the class) or at an attribute level for individual instances or for specific instances (such as all class instances that have an integer value attribute in a range or string attributes in alphabetical ranges). With the design of an attribute, con-tained in a class, a cloud database has the flexibility to model any business process as well as to provide security and the ability to audit access.

A class, then, is a way to identify the attributes contained in a cloud database—and there can be any number of classes. A class can also have active processes running for all instances of the class and maintain policies for all instances; or each instance of the class can maintain policies and run processes for an instance; or individual attributes can run processes and have discrete policies as well. What is important—aside from the flexibility—is that each and every instance of a class or each individual attribute, and its value, can live in the cloud safely.

Perimeter Security

Why is it necessary to be so detailed in the protection scheme for data in the cloud? The answer relates to security perimeters. In the enterprise or produc-tion systems owned and operated by a company, a perimeter encompasses networks of computers controlled by firewalls or other network equipment. It is relatively easy to audit such configurations because the devices are directly accessible, and the only configuration belongs to the organization. In the cloud, the perimeter is lost—specifically in Platform as a Service (PaaS) and Software as a Service (SaaS) deployments—due to multitenancy. A customer can configure security to their cloud services; however, the services are shared with other customers and the containment is lost.

The perimeter is now at the data level. The applications managing the data are also on shared servers, so containment and accuracy in audit-related findings is no longer granular enough to make decisions in an audit report. The data is left alone, potentially across many data centers, and needs to be contained to the customer who has to manage and protect the data. In order to have auditability and security in the cloud, protection must be at the data level.

Another benefit to data-level protection, aside from the protection itself, is the ability to easily move data to other cloud environments for disaster recovery needs. In an enterprise that wants to maintain business continuity, data that protects itself can easily be moved to another cloud provider without having to apply a variety of security or other processes prior to or after a move to a disaster recovery location. Data that protects and monitors itself simply drops into a new cloud storage environment and is ready to be used.

CRYPTOGRAPHIC PROTECTION OF THE DATA

Cryptographic protection of data in the cloud is problematic, as well. Cryptography requires access to keys in order to provide the protection scheme required, and maintaining the keys in the cloud is an issue. If the cloud were to be breached in some way, the keys would also be compromised. In order to avoid this type of breach, the keys used to protect the data should be maintained by the enterprise or customer in their own environments, or a key management cloud should be used. A key management cloud maintains keys for the cryptographic operations needed in the cloud storage environment and are fetched whenever the keys are needed or another cloud can be constructed to perform cryptographic operations on data.

Data protection can render data unsearchable. In the case where an attribute value is needed as a key, as an index for searching, or as data collation, the attribute value can be exposed in a protected form. The search or collation operations can then understand the protection scheme and allow any data-oriented operation to work and still be protected.

Many of the ideas for protection and business operations on protected data exist today and can be used off-the-shelf.

Lastly, from a strictly audit-related perspective, each data attribute in the new cloud storage mechanism can provide its own audit trail. As discussed earlier, the audit capability can exist at the aggregate attribute value level, at the object instance level, or at the class level.

Each instance of object storage environment access can result in an audit trail, which is protected from tampering and can also be stored in a different cloud storage environment. Reporting products can be used to view the audit trail for object access manually or by way of an automated process. Access to objects in the cloud, which fail access control or other policies, can also be sent to security monitoring products and services such as a security operations center. An audit trail, which is itself protected, can be used to demonstrate levels of due care, and an auditor can review processes and reports for their findings.

One of the audit processes that can be maintained by a class, object instances, and attribute values is the geographic location of the data. There are techniques and products that can be used to geo-locate where in the world a cloud storage environment exists. Also, because it is a process maintained with the data, it can produce an audit trail that can be used to report and create security incidents under specific geographic location policies.

IN SUMMARY

It's all about the data. Cloud storage needs to be morphed in order to enable security but also to allow an audit to be conducted to ensure compliance with regulatory requirements.

The nature of cloud storage today is that it depends on the customer to provide the level of security required. These customer requirements range from data protection to data location. Data location is important for privacy requirements given government requirements to protect citizen data.

The morphology discussed in this chapter is a part of active research within the Trusted Cloud Initiative and is also derived from Cloud Security Alliance guidance and also follows the ideas in the CloudAudit 1.0 project.

The data storage currently available for clouds does not possess the capabilities outlined in this chapter. There are some cloud storage providers that allow for appropriate geographic location; however, a customer must know how to enable that feature. The existing cloud storage capabilities do not take into account granular protection or audit capability.

Given the inconsistency of cloud storage protection and audit capabilities, there is a need to create a new cloud storage capability to enable global data protection and regulatory audit capability that is automated and allow for agile enterprise adoption of cloud environments.

Finally, the cloud storage morphology ideas in the chapter further enable incident response and disaster recovery programs. Data-level security enables many aspects of security, audit, and business capability in the cloud.

Cloud Computing Audit Checklist

Jeff Fenton

THIS APPENDIX CONTAINS a high-level audit checklist based on selected key points introduced throughout the book. More detail on each aspect here can be found in the corresponding chapters.

Cloud-Based IT Audit Process (Chapter 2)

☐ Has the organization applied overall risk management governance to the cloud-provided services? Have relevant risks been identified and treated, including the consideration of insurance where appropriate?

☐ Has legal counsel been engaged to evaluate provider contracts and address data protection, confidentiality, and intellectual property issues? Have issues such as source code escrow for provided applications been addressed? What if there is a change in control of the cloud provider?

☐ When an existing, internally hosted system is moved to the cloud, have the controls that were provided internally but are not provided in the cloud been identified? When the system was developed internally and is later moved to the cloud, which controls did developers assume or develop that are not provided in the cloud?

❑ How will generic patching and testing practices at the cloud provider impact custom systems moved to the cloud?

❑ What additional endpoint security measures will be needed once clients access systems in the cloud rather than endpoints behind enterprise gateway controls (firewall, anti-malware, anti-spam, etc.) accessing internal systems?

❑ More generally, how are controls being moved closer to the cloud-hosted system and its data because overall controls within an enterprise cannot be applied in the cloud?

❑ What identity management, authentication, authorization, and access controls are in place in the cloud, and how will they be audited?

❑ How will issues of communication latency, breach notification, and privacy laws/regulations be addressed?

❑ Has relevant external guidance been applied (it may include the FedRAMP Program for cloud providers to the U.S. government, European Network and Information Security Agency Risk Assessment, Information Security Audit & Control Association, and the Cloud Security Alliance [CSA] Controls Matrix)?

❑ Have core control areas been identified (see Exhibit 2.1)?

❑ Have standard audit issues been considered, including auditor independence, auditor technical proficiency and professional practices, and audit reports that clearly present findings and qualified opinions based on evidence?

Cloud-Based IT Governance (Chapter 3)

❑ Is an overall information security governance framework in place in the organization? Does the organization understand the criticality of the information it collects, stores, and processes? Are information security investments and program activities aligned with the organization's strategy, risk profile, and business needs? Is there a top-level information security governance committee representing senior management, key business stakeholders, IT management, Audit, and Risk and Compliance to assist the chief information security officer in setting direction for the information security program? Is the information security program's effectiveness regularly reviewed?

❑ Does the organization have a written information security policy representing senior management's commitment? Are all personnel required to acknowledge their responsibilities to protect the organization's information resources?

☐ Has the organization followed a Governance Implementation and Continuous Improvement Methodology (see Exhibit 3.1) and extended it to governance of cloud computing initiatives?

☐ Does the governance committee review service-level agreements for cloud services?

System and Infrastructure Life Cycle Management for the Cloud (Chapter 4)

☐ Has the organization identified suitable controls based on mitigating known risks? Is the cost of implementing each control proportional to the cost of exposure? What if the control itself fails? Has the organization anticipated and evaluated unknown risks?

☐ Has the organization applied well-known control frameworks (ITIL, COBIT, CSA, NIST) as a starting point?

☐ How will the organization verify that controls are in place and operating properly: by direct verification, control attestations, or certification of the cloud provider to standards? Has the organization considered the advantages and disadvantages of a right-to-audit clause?

Cloud-Based IT Service Delivery and Support (Chapter 5)

☐ Does the cloud provider offering provide true multitenancy, as distinguished from legacy models such as managed service providers and application service providers?

☐ Does the cloud provider offer granular privilege management across all data elements in a multitenant environment?

☐ What logging and reporting capabilities does the provider offer?

☐ What choices on storage location and encryption does the provider offer?

Protection and Privacy of Information Assets in the Cloud (Chapter 6)

☐ Has the organization evaluated the best fit of cloud deployment and service model based on its information protection and privacy needs (see Exhibit 6.6)?

☐ Has the organization categorized data according to its sensitivity and the privacy and protection needs associated with levels of sensitivity?

☐ Does the organization understand its inventory of data elements based on data producer, data consumer, and sensitivity, along with the life cycle of each?

☐ Has the organization assessed the confidentiality, integrity, availability, and accountability needs for each data element at rest and in flight?

☐ Has the organization applied this understanding to create a Cloud Information Protection and Privacy Specification (see Exhibit 6.9)?

Business Continuity and Disaster Recovery (Chapter 7)

☐ Does the organization have an overall Business Continuity Planning (BCP) program and an IT Disaster Recovery Planning (DRP) program integrated with BCP through supporting the organization's critical business processes?

☐ Has the organization considered cloud services to implement or augment traditional DRP activities?

☐ Has the organization assessed the BCP and DRP controls at the cloud provider, based on the CSA recommendations?

☐ Has the organization considered issues such as retrieving its data in case the cloud provider suffers a disruption, arranging for a backup cloud provider, and verifying that the cloud provider's own DR plan is tested?

Global Regulation and Cloud Computing (Chapter 8)

☐ Has the organization identified the laws, regulations, and standards that apply to its business in each country or other jurisdiction in which it operates?

☐ Will the cloud provider offer assurances that it can meet regulatory requirements and be audited by the customer organization or a third party for verification of controls?

☐ Has the organization involved its audit management function in cloud computing plans from the outset?

☐ As part of the service-level agreement, what arrangements are in place for the cloud provider to notify the customer organization in case of a suspected breach? What arrangements for logging and forensic investigation are in place? Would the provider support the investigation?

☐ Has the organization considered the geographic location of data stored at cloud providers in terms of privacy and export control regulations? Will the cloud provider guarantee storage of the organization's data in a particular country?

Cloud Morphing: Shaping the Future of Cloud Computing Security and Audit (Chapter 9)

☐ Have the organization and the cloud provider considered applying the CSA's CloudAudit initiative?

☐ How are security controls such as firewalls, intrusion detection, patch management, and anti-malware granularly applied to virtual environments at the cloud provider?

☐ Does the cloud provider associate policy attributes to each data element it stores and apply this metadata approach to facilitate the application of controls? Does each data element generate its own audit trail?

☐ Does the customer organization maintain control of encryption keys or use a separate cloud to manage encryption keys?

About the Editor

Ben Halpert is the Director of Information Technology Risk Management and Compliance at McKesson Corporation. In his off-hours, he is a champion for the protection of children in cyberspace.

Seeing a void in the conversation about online safety for children before they begin K to 12, Ben created a nonprofit to represent those who cannot speak for themselves: infants, toddlers, and preschool children. Savvy Cyber Kids, Inc., was founded in 2007 to fill the education gap. Ben authored the children's picture book *The Savvy Cyber Kids At Home: The Family Gets A Computer*, which was released in October, 2010. His next book, *The Savvy Cyber Kids At Home: The Defeat of the Cyber Bully*, is due out in late 2011.

Ben was a contributing author to *Readings and Cases in the Management of Information Security* and the *Encyclopedia of Information Ethics and Security*. Ben is the security columnist for *Mobile Enterprise Magazine* and has contributed to seven NIST special publications. Ben is on the advisory board of numerous colleges and universities. He has keynoted and presented sessions at numerous conferences, including the RSA Security Conference, InfoSec World, IEEE, and ACM conferences. Ben is an adjunct instructor at a local university where he teaches the master's of IT information security concentration curriculum. Ben is a Certified Information Systems Security Professional (CISSP) and holds two master's degrees.

About the Contributors

Omkhar Arasaratnam is the Lead Security Architect for a number of cloud computing solutions at IBM. With over 10 years of experience at IBM, he has held a variety of security-related roles, including running the Ethical Hacking team, and serving as interim Chief Information Security Officer for a number of IBM clients. He exhibits a unique combination of deep technical skills paired with a keen business acumen, and has advised the C-suite of IBM's largest customers on how to successfully position security as a business enabler.

Mr. Arasaratnam co-leads The Open Group Cloud Working Group's Security for the Cloud and SOA project, and is the worldwide leader for IBM's cloud submissions at the ISO's JTC1/SC38. He is also an accomplished author and technical editor of several IBM and O'Reilly publications. Mr. Arasaratnam is an IBM Certified IT Architect, and an Open Group Certified Master Architect.

Jeremy Rissi joined Triton Federal Solutions in 2009 to develop sales strategy and new business for the PPC subsidiary. A 10-year veteran of several high-growth technology companies, he brings his enthusiasm and creativity to government customers seeking to design and build complex systems. Mr. Rissi has a track record of successfully selling innovative solutions, from some of the first automated workflow systems delivered by his team at webMethods, to data center password automation deployed at the CDC and Pacific Northwest National Labs by Cloakware, to mobility solutions designed by Trust Digital for SPAWAR and the Air Force.

Mr. Rissi grew up on an island off the coast of Maine and earned a BA in History at Yale University. He lives in Alexandria, Virginia, with his wife, Erika, and their daughters, Anna Luiza and Sophia. When not working with leading-edge technology, he is an accomplished concert cellist and an active volunteer and nonprofit board member.

Sean Sherman is a Senior Security Consultant working for clients to provide strategic security and compliance solutions and solve complex problems to balance risk, compliance, and security.

With over 24 years of IT experience, Mr. Sherman has seen the security and IT industry through many changes. He is active in the security and audit field, and has recently finished tenure as president of his local ISACA chapter.

Mr. Sherman is considered a subject matter expert for a number of current compliance, security, and privacy programs, including: NERC, NIST/FISMA, CNSS, ISO 27001, PCI, HIPAA, GLBA, SOX, and other current IT security regulations and frameworks. His background includes working over 10 years in the Federal IT/Security space, including significant work with FISMA, smart grid cyber security, classified systems development, and compliance/governance efforts. He holds a variety of certifications, including CISA, CISSP, PMP, MCSE, CIPP, and CPISM.

Assistant Professor **Herb Mattord**, CISM, CISSP, CDP, currently teaches undergraduate courses in Information Security and Assurance and Information Systems. He is the Operations Manager of the Kennesaw State University (KSU) Center for Information Security Education (infosec.kennesaw.edu), as well as the coordinator for the KSU Department of Computer Science and Information Systems Certificate in Information Security and Assurance.

He completed 24 years of IT industry experience before becoming a full-time academic in 2002. His experiences as an application developer, database administrator, project manager, and information security practitioner are a valuable background to his teaching role at Kennesaw State University. While engaged in his IT career, he worked as an adjunct professor at KSU in Kennesaw, Georgia; Southern Polytechnic State University in Marietta, Georgia; Austin Community College in Austin, Texas; and Texas State University-San Marcos. He was formerly the Manager of Corporate Information Technology Security at Georgia-Pacific Corporation, where his practical knowledge of information security implementation and management was acquired.

Mr. Mattord is the co-author with Dr. Michael Whitman of *Principles of Information Security 4th Edition*; *Management of Information Security 3rd Edition*; *Principles of Incident Response and Disaster Recovery, Readings and Cases in the Management of Information Security: Law and Ethics, Readings and Cases in the Management of Information Security: Volume II: Legal and Ethical Issues, Roadmap to Information Security for IT and InfoSec managers*; and *Hands-On Information Security Lab Manual, 3rd Edition*.

He is also currently enrolled in the PhD in Information Systems program at Nova Southeastern University.

Michael E. Whitman, PhD, CISM, CISSP is a professor of Information Security at Kennesaw State University (KSU), with over 10 years' experience designing and implementing information security courses. He has authored several textbooks in information security including: *Principles of Information Security*, 4th edition; *Management of Information Security*, 3rd edition; *Principles of Incident Response and Disaster Recovery*; *Readings and Cases in the Management of Information Security, Volumes I and II*; *Hands-On Information Security Lab Manual*, 3rd edition; *Guide to Firewalls and Network Security: With Intrusion Detection and VPNs*, 2nd edition. Dr. Whitman is an active researcher in information security, fair and responsible use policies, and ethical computing and information systems research methods. He has published articles in *Information Systems Research*, the *Communications of the ACM*, *Information and Management*, the *Journal of International Business Studies*, and the *Journal of Computer Information Systems*. He is a member of the Information Systems Security Association, the Association for Computing Machinery, and the Association for Information Systems.

Steve Riley is Technical Leader in the office of the CTO at Riverbed Technology, an innovator in wide-area networking and storage optimization. Steve actively works to raise awareness of the technical and business benefits of Riverbed's solutions, particularly as they relate to accelerating the enterprise adoption of cloud computing. His specialties include information security, compliance, privacy, and policy. Mr. Riley has spoken at hundreds of events around the world, including RSA, SANS, Black Hat Windows, InfoSec US, (ISC) 2, SIIA, IANS, TechEd, Connections, Cloud Expo, and Interop. He co-authored a book about Windows network security, has published numerous articles, and has conducted technical reviews of several data networking and tele-communications books. Born with an Ethernet cable attached to his belly button, He grew up in networking and telecommunications. Besides lurking in the Internet's dark alleys and secret passages, he enjoys freely sharing his opinions about the intersection of technology and culture. Contact him at stvrly@gmail.com, on Skype as stvrly, and join the conversation at http://stvrly.tumblr.com.

Peter Coffee is a corporate Vice President with salesforce.com, Inc., serving as the company's Head of Platform Research. He joined the company in January 2007 after spending 18 years as a senior contributor to the enterprise technology journals *eWEEK* and *PC Week*. Based in the Los Angeles area, he works with IT professionals and independent developers to build a global community based on Force.com: the salesforce.com Platform Cloud.

Mr. Coffee has 28 years' experience in guiding the introduction and adoption of new technologies and practices as a developer, consultant, educator, and internationally published author and lecturer. He has assisted major media outlets throughout the United States, Latin America, and Asia in addressing a broad range of eBusiness issues. He chaired the four-day Web Security Summit conference in Boston during the summer of 2000; he has been a keynote speaker, moderator, and workshop leader at technical conferences, business computing events, and academic gatherings throughout the United States and in India, Singapore, Australia, China, Korea, Canada, Mexico, Brazil, the United Kingdom, Spain, Italy, and the Netherlands.

He was previously the first Manager of Desktop Computing Integration at The Aerospace Corporation, where he also worked in space systems project management and in space-asset applications of artificial intelligence techniques. Before that, he was a Lead Cost Engineer for arctic project planning, chemical facility construction, and alternative-fuels engineering efforts at various units of Exxon Corporation in New Jersey, Louisiana, California, and Alaska's Beaufort Sea. He holds an engineering degree from MIT and an MBA from Pepperdine University, where he also served as an instructor for graduate classes in IT management; he has held faculty appointments in computer science (artificial intelligence) at UCLA and in business analytics at Chapman College. He is the author of two books: *How To Program Java* and *Peter Coffee Teaches PCs*.

Nikhil Kumar is a technologist and entrepreneur, with over two decades of experience in the IT industry, who loves to innovate and create actionable solutions.

Having worked at organizations such as Price Waterhouse, and with a background in engineering and computer science, Mr. Kumar combines extensive experience with a deep understanding of the underlying technology. He has been living his dream, designing computer architectures and building his company, ApTSi (Applied Technology Solutions, Inc.), with customers in the banking, insurance, financial services, wealth management, and health care sectors. He has contributed to a number of SOA standards; has published on service-oriented, enterprise architecture, security, information and cloud computing and aspect-oriented programming; and is co-chair of the SOA reference architecture project for the Open Group, and on the Board of Trustees at Henry Ford Health Systems. At ApTSi, he is engaged in building its SOA and cloud computing product stacks, as well as consulting with specific clients.

Mr. Kumar lives in South Eastern Michigan with his wife and two children and spends his spare time gardening, bird-watching, and coaching robotics.

Leon DuPree, a consultant with the heart of a teacher and a Doctoral Fellow at the Eastern Michigan University's Center of Excellence for Regional and National Security, has a passion for academic research in the areas of information assurance.

He is currently pursuing research in the field of cloud computing with respect to privacy and the potential inputs and outputs for audit and controls of this changing landscape. As a Fellow in the College of Technology, he has written papers on the areas of "Remote Computer Forensics," "Security Awareness Anxiety," and "Water Mark Validation in Online Banking." Pending grants include NSF Proposal "Cloud Based Computing—Expanding Community Architecture" and "Homeland Security—Infrastructure Risk Management Awareness."

With over 15 years of experience in IT consulting with such firms as Deloitte & Touche and PricewaterhouseCoopers, Mr. DuPree has held positions such as systems engineer, project manager, systems manager, and lead consultant.

He is originally from western New York and lives in Southeastern Michigan with his wife and kids.

Jeff Fenton is a Senior Staff Information Assurance Engineer with a major Fortune 500 company, responsible for information security policy and standards. His security experience also includes business continuity and disaster recovery planning, external network connections, risk management, and security education. His earlier assignments included network design, telecommunications project management, and emergency communications management. He also served as the network operations group leader for one of the company's largest facilities.

Mr. Fenton holds a BA in Economics from the University of California, San Diego; an MA in Economics and an MS in Operations Research from Stanford University; and an MBA in Telecommunications from Golden Gate University. He is a Certified Information Systems Security Professional (CISSP), Certified Information System Security Engineering Professional (ISSEP), Certified Information System Security Management Professional (ISSMP), and a Certified Information Security Manager (CISM). He also holds the SysAdmin, Audit, and Network Security (SANS) Institute's Global Information Assurance Certification (GIAC) in Business Law and Computer Security (GBLC) and the Certified Business Continuity Professional (CBCP) certification from the Disaster Recovery Institute International.

Liam Lynch is a 25-year veteran of the information security industry. He has worked in many areas for information security from military, government, health care, and e-commerce, to name a few.

For the last nine years, Mr. Lynch has been working in e-commerce, starting as the Chief Security Architect for the world's largest e-commerce company, eBay. Over the course of these nine years, He has been responsible for security architecture for technology conversions to adopt Sarbanes-Oxley and PCI compliance, as well as the creator of several patents in the e-commerce security space. Today, He is Chief Security Strategist at eBay and is an active and a founding member of the Cloud Security Alliance and the leader of the Trusted Cloud Initiative.

Tammi Hayes is currently President and Founder of Capital Strategies Group, LLC. Capital Strategies Group is a boutique technology consulting firm, with a primary focus on business development, strategic partnering, and structuring financial transactions. The company specializes in executive level business development and sales, structuring strategic partnerships and financial transactions, raising venture capital, and developing relationships, both business-to-business and business-to-government. Capital Strategies Group was founded by Ms. Hayes in 1998 and is based in Boston, Massachusetts. Clients include PGP, RSA, Pacific Crest, McAfee, Symantec, Nitro Security, Liquid Machines Tenix, Good Technology, eBay, AOL, China.com, Mitsubishi Research Institute, Fairhaven Capital, Sulmona Capital, ANX, State Street Bank, GlassHouse Technologies, Microsoft, UNISYS, E*TRADE, and Trust Digital, to name a few. Tammi has strong executive-level relationships within both the commercial and public sectors, as well as with analysts, venture funds, and investment banks.

Tammi was formerly a Principal at Good Harbor Consulting, a Washington, DC-based strategic consulting firm focused on the fast developing areas of homeland security, cyber security, critical infrastructure protection and counterterrorism. Tammi has over 15 years experience in business development and strategic consulting. Prior to joining Good Harbor, she was a Director at RSA Security, where she led the development and success of a new business unit within RSA focused on consumer services. Tammi has advised various global companies on domestic and international regulatory and policy-related issues. Tammi has also worked extensively overseas in Eastern Europe, Asia, and Africa. While working in South Africa and London, she wrote *African Capital Markets*, which was purchased by investors worldwide. Over the past several years, Ms. Hayes has conducted negotiations between several U.S. companies and foreign ventures. Her expertise lies in structuring strategic partnerships and financial transactions, raising venture capital, and business development. Tammi is also a member of the Executive Women in Security Forum and she is a frequent speaker on cyber-related issues.

In January 2000, Ms. Hayes founded and managed Futuris Capital, LLC, with partners at top investment banks on Wall Street for the purpose of raising seed capital for high-tech Internet, security, and infrastructure-related companies. Futuris Capital is a fund comprised of individual private equity investors from the top-tier investment banks. Ms. Hayes was instrumental in Futuris Capital's $7.25 million private equity investment in a Virginia-based smart card development company, which was subsequently acquired by a large public IT security company.

Ms. Hayes received a BA in Russian Language, Literature, and Culture and a BA in International Relations from Syracuse University. She studied at Moscow State University in 1989 as an undergraduate, received her MA in International Business *cum laude*, and studied at the University of Nairobi in Kenya, Africa, in 1993 to 1994, as well as at Georgetown University. Ms. Hayes has traveled extensively throughout Eastern Europe, Western Europe, Africa, and Asia. She speaks Russian, French, Spanish, and Swahili.

Index

Printed and bound by CPI Group (UK) Ltd, Croydon, CR0 4YY

27/10/2024

14580313-0002